Please return / renew by date shown.
You can renew it at:

N9

RAILMOTOR

The Steam Engine that Rewrote Railway History

ROBIN JONES

Halsgrove

First published in Great Britain in 2011.

Copyright © Robin Jones 2011.

To Jenny, Vicky and Ross

British Library Cataloguing-in-Publication Data
A CIP record for this title is available from the British Library

ISBN 978 0 85704 122 7

HALSGROVE
Halsgrove House,
Ryelands Business Park,
Bagley Road, Wellington, Somerset TA21 9PZ
Tel: 01823 653777   Fax: 01823 216796
email: sales@halsgrove.com

Part of the Halsgrove group of companies
Information on all Halsgrove titles is available at: www.halsgrove.com

Printed and bound by Grafiche Flaminia, Italy

CONTENTS

Grateful thanks are due to Paul Bennett, Michael Collins, Anthony Coulls, Frank Dumbleton, Robert Gardiner, Fred Kerr, Adrian Knowles, Graham Drew, Michael Mensing, Stephen Middleton, Brian Sharpe, Laurence Waters.

Richard Croucher in the railmotor with a leaflet advertising the 1908 Olympic Games, to which No. 93 may have carried spectators. FRANK DUMBLETON

FOREWORD

IN MARCH 2011, Great Western Railway steam railmotor No. 93 re-entered traffic 103 years almost to the day since it first took to the rails from Southall on 9 March 1908. As we contemplate the year 2012 at the time of writing, it is amazing to think that working local services around West London, No. 93 could almost certainly have been used to carry people to the first London Olympics.

During the next 26 years, No. 93 worked all over the GWR covering almost half a million miles. It was amongst the last batch of steam railmotors to be withdrawn in 1934 whereupon it was rebuilt as auto-trailer No. 212 and continued to work a further 20 years.

Then fate took a hand and instead of being cut up it was converted into a mobile office finally being stood-down at the beginning of the 1970s.

Once again fate took a hand, with the Great Western Society acquiring this 'unique' coach in the hope that one day it might be rebuilt and restored as a steam railmotor.

And there matters lay until the early 1990s when the GWS resurrected the idea. Thanks to painstaking research by society member the late Ralph Tutton, it was discovered that there were a large number of drawings of steam railmotors still in existence, sufficient to be able to build a new power bogie based on the original drawings and work began in 1998 on the construction.

The introduction of the steam railmotor is a key milestone in the evolution of the railway system. For the first time, it was no longer necessary for the locomotive to change ends every time it reached a terminus. The driver could just walk from one end of the train to the other and drive off with consequent efficiency savings.

In his book, Robin Jones highlights the important part that the introduction of the steam railmotor as well as the petrol-engined railmotors played in changing railway operations and he traces the development and evolution of the concept through the twentieth century to today's diesel and electric multiple units, which form the backbone of mainline services not only in Britain but most other countries around the world.

The ancestry of today's most successful self-propelled trains can be traced right back to the humble steam railmotor and the restoration of GWR No. 93 can rightly be regarded as a crucial addition to Britain's railway heritage.

The story will be complete with the restoration of auto-trailer No. 92, at which point the railmotor becomes part of a genuine Steam Multiple Unit.

Richard Croucher – Chairman, Great Western Society, Didcot Railway Centre
August 2011

The picture that underlines the huge heritage and educational importance of GWR steam railmotor No. 93: six generations and 100 years of development of drive-from-each-end trains are lined up at Didcot on 28 May 2011: left to right are No. 93, built in 1908; an auto-train comprising 1444 class locomotive No. 4866 and auto-trailer which replaced the railmotors by the 1930s; an example of their successors, GWR diesel railcar No. 22 of 1940; a Chiltern Railways Class 121 'bubblecar' of 1960; a First Great Western Class 166 Turbotrain of the 1990s, and a new Class 172 for Chiltern Railways, delivered just two days before and yet to carry a passenger. FRANK DUMBLETON

Britain's greatest new-build locomotive projects came together for the first time at the steam railmotor's Didcot Railway Centre home on 11 June 2011, when No. 93 lined up alongside the £3-million Peppercorn A1 Pacific No. 60163 Tornado. FRANK DUMBLETON

CHAPTER ONE
THE STEAM ENGINE THAT REWROTE RAILWAY HISTORY

DURING MY CAREER as a railway magazine editor, there is precious little that has come my way that has not been written about before. The railway sector ranks as one of the biggest subjects by far as far as popular history is concerned, and in the ever-rising mountain of books on the subject, there are so many mainstream areas that have been covered time and time again that there surely cannot be anything new to say about them, other to empty old wine into new bottles.

Once in a lifetime, however, emerges a topic that is truly different from the rest. In most cases, it is often the restoration of an obscure industrial locomotive, maybe the rediscovery of the remains of a long-buried early railway, or perhaps some archive documents which throw fresh light on the dawn of steam.

Yet what happens when a largely-forgotten form of traction, not a model or miniature

Restored GWR steam railmotor No. 93 in an evocative scene after dark at Llangollen, 24 March 2011. The Chalford destination board recalls the early steam railmotor services in the Stroud valley. ADRIAN KNOWLES

version, reappears in its as-built glory from a century ago, not only giving us a window into an earlier railway age, but having a unique capacity to change the way in which we view railways as popular history, and our understanding of how the steam age evolved into today's sleek and streamlined diesel and electric national network? In red-top newspaper terms, a true sensation, the Rosetta stone of the railway sector.

This is the story of Great Western Railway steam railmotor No. 93, which reappeared phoenix-like in 2011 and has the ability to rewrite popular railway history.

Take the ordinary man in the street, the non-enthusiast painting a modestly-informed broad brush stroke when asked about the development of railways. George Stephenson's *Rocket* was the first steam engine, successive engineers developed it and honed it to perfection, *Flying Scotsman* marked the zenith of the steam era, along came Dr Beeching and replaced the dirty grimy steam engines with sleek new diesel and electric locomotives, and gave us the railway network of today.

All well and good, but the steam railway locomotive was invented by Cornish mining engineer Richard Trevithick a quarter of a century before *Rocket* appeared. True, the design of *Rocket* was a defining watershed in the evolution of the steam locomotive, and in May 1904, the Great Western Railway's 4-4-0 *City of Truro* may have broken the 100mph barrier. *Flying Scotsman* officially performed that feat 30 years later.

In an everyday scene on today's rail network, East Midlands Trains Class 222 DMU No. 222.011 passes a Class 125 High Speed Train headed by Class 43 power car No 43076 at Leicester on July 1 2011. Both sets and many other types on today's network have the steam railmotor as their direct ancestor. ROBIN JONES

Once the years of postwar austerity began to thin out, British Railways looked to replace steam haulage by diesel and electric traction, a process well underway in other countries like the USA, on the continent and closer to home, Ireland. The mass public switch from rail to road as the price of motor vehicles came down, an inevitable trend because of the greater versatility that the car, van and lorry offers especially in terms of individual choice, spurred the rail network to respond through modernisation. In Britain, the panic in the late fifties to dispense with steam led to several types of diesel locomotive being produced which failed to pass muster in the medium to long term and some of them were withdrawn from service even before their steam counterparts. Many diesel locomotive types were hugely successful – the Class 37s and

47s, for example and the glamorous Deltics which replaced the Pacifics on the East Coast Main Line, the route of the *Flying Scotsman*.

Yet today, very few passenger trains in Britain, and indeed in many other countries, are hauled by locomotives. The vast bulk of modern trains are made up of DMUs (diesel multiple units), which are self-powered, or EMUs (electric multiple units), which draw power from either an overhead supply or a third rail alongside the track.

The biggest advantage of this form of train is that driving cabs are located at both ends. There is no need for a locomotive to uncouple and 'run round' its train when it reaches its destination; neither is a turntable required to place the train locomotive in the forward direction. Indeed, if the terminus in question never handles locomotive-hauled trains or freight workings, you can eliminate the run-round loop altogether, boosting efficiency while cutting costs.

While history has recorded the dazzling speed feats of the GWR Castle and Kings and the great LNER Pacifics, stuff that schoolboy annual legends are made of, they did not address the versatility problem. No matter what timing they set, what record they broke, they still had to be turned and run round at each end.

The real future of the railways lay in a far more humble form of traction, the steam railmotor, in effect a carriage with a steam engine built into it, that can be controlled from either end.

Thanks to the efforts of the Great Western Society which acquired the remains of the last existing GWR railmotor body, that of No. 93, in 2011 we saw it run again after an absence of 77 years. Now unique in Britain, it has with vast justification staked its claim to be the true missing link between the age of steam and the modern network of today.

EARLY ALTERNATIVES TO STEAM LOCOMOTIVES

It is also a common misconception today that following the development of *Rocket* and its victory at the Rainhill Trials of 1829, the steam locomotive was enshrined as the only way ahead for rail transport.

Not so. Marc Brunel and his son Isambard, the future GWR engineer, experimented unsuccessfully for several years with the their Gaz engine as a potential rival form of traction, while in 1838, when gas engineer Samuel Clegg and marine engineers Jacob and Joseph Samuda patented "a new improvement in valves", atmospheric propulsion became possible.

The first practical use of the atmospheric railway system, which effectively saw carriages pulled along by a vacuum in a pipe between the rails, with stationary steam engines positioned at regular intervals along the line to create the vacuum, was on the Dublin & Kingstown Railway's 1.75-mile Dalkey Atmospheric Railway between 1844-54.

It impressed Isambard Brunel so much that he adopted the Samuda system for his South

Great Western Railway engineer Isambard Kingdom Brunel tried to break the conventional steam engine mould by introducing locomotive-less trains on his short-lived South Devon atmospheric railway, seen here at Dawlish. IRONBRIDGE GORGE MUSEUM TRUST

Devon Railway, locomotive-less trains running between 13 September 1847 and 9 September 1848 and achieving some extremely impressive speeds, but the system could not be maintained due to the inadequacy of supporting technologies such as materials, and so was quickly scrapped in favour of by-then traditional steam locomotive haulage.

It was not until the 1880s that a serious alternative to steam railways arrived in Britain. Following experiments in the USA and Germany, Brighton inventor Magnus Volk opened Britain's first electric railway, on the town's seafront on 4 August 1883. Volk's Electric Railway is still very much in operation today, as the oldest surviving electric railway in the world, and the ancestor of today's electric locomotives and electric multiple units.

TWO ENDS ARE BETTER THAN ONE

A 'halfway house' solution to the abovementioned operational drawbacks of rail-mounted traction was presented by engineer Robert Francis Fairlie: join two steam engines back to back, and you never have to use a turntable.

Fairlie's first double-ended locomotive, *Pioneer*, was built by James Cross & Co. of St Helens supplied to the standard gauge Neath & Brecon Railway in 1865, but it was not successful. However, *Little Wonder*, built in 1869 for the 1ft 11½in gauge Festiniog Railway in Snowdonia, turned the corner for Fairlie fame and fortune.

On 11 February 1870 at the Festiniog (originally spelled with one 'f'), Fairlie hosted a meeting of locomotive engineers as far afield at Russia, Mexico, Turkey and Sweden. There, he demonstrated *Little Wonder*, and was left with a mountain of orders. By 1876, 43 different

railways had operated his double-ended locomotives.

However, the only places where the double-ended steam engines remained in use in the long term were Mexico, New Zealand and the Festiniog. A fleet of 49 giant 0-6-0+0-6-0s were used in Mexico until the 1920s. The drawbacks were the limited capacity for fuel and water, the flexible steam pipes being prone to leakage and wasting of power and the absence of unpowered wheels to act as stabilisers.

Nonetheless, the concept of a 'double ended' train had been well and truly established. We may gaze in wonder at the double Fairlies on the Ffestiniog Railway today, but are not most modern diesel and electric locomotives, shunters apart, equipped with cabs at both ends? Yet while turntables and turning triangles have been eliminated, there is still the need for run-round loops, the associated signalling and the space they take up.

Once the steam passenger railway had been established, someone, somewhere, would inevitably ask the obvious question – why not design an all-in-one unit that needs neither a turntable nor a run-round loop?

A complete passenger train that could be controlled from both ends, in which all the driver has to do to turn round is walk from one end of the vehicle to another?

That person was William Bridges Adams, the father of the steam railmotor.

David Lloyd George, *a modern-day double Fairlie replica built by the Ffestiniog Railway in 1982.* ROBIN JONES

Little Wonder, *the hugely-successful double Fairlie locomotive, in action on the Festiniog Railway.* FR

DECADES AHEAD OF HIS TIME

Born in Woore, Staffordshire, Adams became apprenticed to the coachbuilding firm of Baxter & Pierce of Long Acre, London. When Napoleon's carriage was brought there after the Battle of Waterloo, young William made a drawing of it.

In December 1819 he married Elizabeth Place, the daughter of social reformer Francis Place, and they set out for South America to make their fortune. He survived the earthquake in Valparaiso, Chile, on 19 November 1822, but Elizabeth died when giving birth to a second child the following year. Adams and his son returned to England and after a trip to the USA, he took a job with coachbuilder Hobson & Co, again in London, and married again twice.

Adams moved from coach-making into railway engineering and set up a business making his patented 'bow springs' for use of both road and railway carriages.

His factory moved to a three-acre site at Fair Field, Bow in East London, adjoining the Eastern Counties Railway, where he founded the Fairfield Locomotive Works in 1843.

His most far-reaching railway inventions were the fishplate, used for joining two sections of rail together, replacing the less satisfactory scarf joints of the day, and his patented Adams Axle, a radial axle design which remained in use on railways in Britain until the end of standard gauge steam traction in 1968.

The Fairfield *Steam Carriage, which ran on the Bristol & Exeter Railway.*
ILLUSTRATED LONDON NEWS

His factory turned out some steam engines and inspection trolleys which were quickly consigned to obscurity. However, more importantly to us, he also produced the first steam railmotors or railcars.

The earliest recorded example was a 12ft 6in long four-wheeled vehicle named *Express* designed by James Samuel and built in 1847 by Adams at Fairfield Works, Bow. Nicknamed *Lilliputian* because of its size, it made its debut run from Shoreditch to Cambridge on the Eastern Counties Railway. Capable of reaching 47mph, it had 40in diameter wheels, and two cylinders 31.2in by 6in. During six months in 1848, it ran for 5,500 miles.

That year, Adams brought a larger Samuel design into reality, a six-wheeled 7ft 0¼in broad gauge vehicle called *Fairfield*. The driving pair of wheels were 54in in diameter, and it had a vertical boiler with cylinders measuring 7in by 12in.

It was tested on the West London Railway late in 1848, although it was in early 1850 that modifications to bring it up to agreed standards were made by Adams.

The Bristol & Exeter Railway, which also had been engineered by Isambard Brunel, used it on the Tiverton and Clevedon branches, and possibly on the short line to Weston-super-Mare itself. It became No. 29 in the BER fleet, but was commonly referred to as 'the Fairfield locomotive'.

The boiler was not covered by a cab or other bodywork. It had seats for 16 first class and 32 second class passengers. It was said to have reach 52mph on one occasion, but overall, the BER was not impressed sufficiently to order a batch. Instead, the company's traction policy veered towards traditional 2-2-2 locomotives.

In 1851 the carriage portion of the Fairfield locomotive was removed and the power unit rebuilt into an 0-2-2 locomotive. It is said that it ended its days in BER service being used to pump water at Taunton, but in 1856 it was sold to engineering contractor Hutchinson and Ritson which was building the Somerset Central Railway. Before delivery, the BER agreed to rebuild it as an 0-4-0, and the £600 price was paid for in prepared timber.

In 1849, Adams turned out an even bigger railcar, one with eight wheels. Named *Enfield*, it operated on the Eastern Counties Railway branch between Enfield and Angel Road. Its driving wheels were 60in in diameter with 8in by 12in cylinders. It was also occasionally used as a locomotive on the main line, and had raised buffers for use with other rolling stock.

Under tests, it made the 126-mile journey from London to Norwich in three hours 35 minutes. However, it was very much a one-off in a world dominated by the straightforward locomotive concept, and it was eventually converted to a conventional 2-2-2 tank engine.

In Ireland, Adams' patent well-tank engines fitted with a small stagecoach-type body came to the attention of the Londonderry & Enniskillen Railway, which obtained one in 1850 and six more in 1852. The Londonderry & Coleraine Railway also acquired one in 1853.

Other manufacturers were watching Adams, although mostly remaining less than

Largely forgotten by history is Robert Fairlie's experimental steam railway carriage. ILLUSTRATED LONDON NEWS

convinced. The famous locomotive builder Kitson of Leeds produced a railcar called *Ariel's Girdle* which was displayed at the Great Exhibition of 1851 in the Crystal Palace.

In August 1869, the *Illustrated London News* carried a report and picture of an early steam carriage being demonstrated on a train-set-like oval of track at Hatcham Ironworks, the headquarters of the Fairlie Engine and Steam Carriage Company, run by none other than Robert Fairlie, he of double-ended locomotives fame. It was the same year that his double Fairlie *Little Wonder* was demonstrated on the Festiniog Railway with overwhelming success.

The report read: "On several occasions the principles of the double-bogie engines and light carriages for railways, advocated and developed with so much perseverance by Mr Fairlie, have been favourably criticised; and recently there was a successful public exhibition of a light steam-carriage for branch lines and lines of small traffic.

"The length of the carriage is 43ft, including a compartment for the guard; the engine, carriage, and framing complete weighs, exclusive of passengers, 13½ tons; and including its load of 66 passengers (16 first class and 50 second), only 18½ tons.

"When entirely completed, it will have a broad step or platform on each side, extending its entire length, and protected by a handrail, to enable the guard to pass completely round the train. Passengers can also pass along it to the guard, affording thus an easy means of intercommunication.

"The engine, running on two pairs of small wheels close together, so as to give the smallest amount of wheel base, forms one bogie, or platform, upon which the front part of the passenger-carriage is supported and pivoted, this carriage having another bogie or platform, to which it is also pivoted, supporting its rear end. There is thus a large freedom of motion, and it was astonishing to witness the speed and grace with which this long body was swung at more than eighteen miles an hour round curves of only 40ft upon an oval line of rails under 200 yards in circumference, laid down in a garden attached to the Hatcham Ironworks.

"Never before has the world seen a railway carriage of such large dimensions with 66 passengers spun round at railway pace in a metropolitan plot of ground of less than three quarters of an acre."

Indeed, with such clear advantages, the modern reader is left wondering why the railway companies of the day did not respond as vigorously to the steam carriage as they did the same year to the double Fairlies, for the concept seemed to have faded away afterwards.

Adams' engineering business failed some years later, although by then he had expanded his commercial empire to include clothing design and journalism.

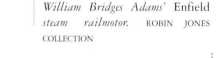

William Bridges Adams' Enfield *steam railmotor.* ROBIN JONES COLLECTION

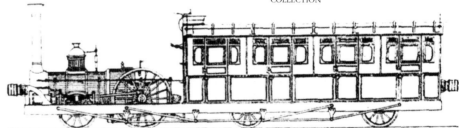

STEAM SPRITES IN LEPRECHAUN COUNTRY

In 1857, Ireland's Great Southern & Western Railway built an early steam railmotor at its Inchicore Works. *Sprite* comprised an 0-2-4 tank engine with small 6½in by 12in cylinders and a single 4ft 6in driving wheels built into a saloon. It was not used for public services, but as an inspection car for company officers, and for the payment of wages at remote stations.

In 1872, it was withdrawn, and replaced the following year by a slightly larger second *Sprite*, an 0-4-4T with the carriage portion purpose-designed as a pay office, with an open rear platform, and utilising the saloon from the original. While this *Sprite* was rebuilt in 1889 as a traditional 0-4-2T with its carriage mounted on a separate frame, in 1894, another pay carriage named *Fairy*, and resembling the second *Sprite*, was built.

Ireland's Midland & Great Western Railway in 1866 converted 2-2-2 No. 33 *Falcon* to a 2-2-4T, with a saloon compartment over the rear bogie coach for about eight persons. Used for inspection purposes, it was withdrawn about 1874 and sold to an unspecified buyer the following year.

The GSWR also produced three "carriage engines" for public services the initially-independent 4½-mile Castleisland Railway which connected the town of Castleisland to a junction at Gortatlea on the Tralee & Killarney Railway, and which opened on 30 August 1875, with 'light' 40lb rail which limited the speed of trains to 20mph and their weight to 6½ tons.

At Inchicore Works, the GSWR designed the first of them, small 0-6-4T with 3ft 8½in diameter wheels and placed it inside a passenger coach body running on a four-wheeled bogie, the frame being rigid throughout. The carriage section comprised an eight-seat first class compartment immediately behind the driver's cab and a guards van that could additionally seat six third-class passengers. However, this vehicle was not built in Ireland, but at the Crewe works of the London & North Western Railway. There, it must have been one of, it not the, smallest locomotive ever built for passenger service.

The first and second versions of Sprite, *of which no known photograph exists.* MICHAEL COLLINS

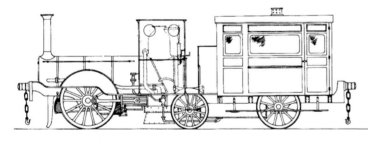

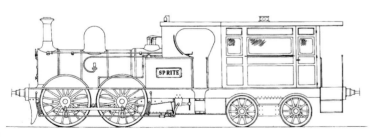

The GSWR bought the Castleisland Railway on 1 May 1879, and built two more of these "carriage engines."

However, the traffic on the line became too great for them to handle, and in 1897 the track was upgraded to allow it to be worked by standard goods locomotives and 0-4-4Ts. The carriage engines were then transferred to the Mitchelstown branch.

Another pair, Nos. 99 and 100, were built for working mixed trains on short branches.

Two of the carriage engines, Nos. 90 and 91, were converted to 'normal' 0-6-0 tank engines at Inchicore in 1915. As an 0-6-0T, No. 90 survived into preservation, and after restoration by the Railway Preservation Society of Ireland, is based at the Downpatrick & County Down Railway. Nobody has seriously suggested back-converting it into its original guise as an early steam railmotor, for that is exactly what the "carriage engines" were.

Great Southern & Western Railway carriage engine No. 92, complete with coach body. It is the same as No. 90, which survives as a tank engine.
NATIONAL RAILWAY MUSEUM

The Great Southern & Western Railway 'pay carriage' Fairy.
MICHAEL COLLINS COLLECTION

19

CHAPTER TWO
THE AGE OF THE RAILMOTOR

FOR HALF A CENTURY after William Bridges Adams, the railmotor concept was all but consigned to the dustbin of history. In a burgeoning sector where locomotive traction was the norm, there was no place for 'one offs'.

Efforts at producing a steam-powered all-in-one vehicle switched from railways to roads as transport technology took giant steps forward. In March 1873, London civil engineer John Grantham demonstrated an experimental 23ft steam-powered double-ended four-wheel open-top tramcar at a railway arch in Salamanca Street, Lambeth.

The mechanism was built by Merryweather & Sons of Greenwich, a firm which built steam fire engines, and the body by Oldbury Railway Carriage & Wagon Works. It held 44 passengers, having seats for 20 inside and 24 on top.

Grantham died in July 1874, but his vehicle entered service on the Wantage Tramway in Oxfordshire on 1 August 1874, becoming Britain's first public steam tram, and lasted in service for 23 years.

However, the major problem with steam trams was the fact that lightly-laid horse tram tracks in the streets could not carry their weight, and eventually electric trams won the day. Railways, however, did not suffer from this disadvantage.

In 1902, Dugald Drummond, locomotive engineer of the London & South Western Railway, rebooted the railmotor concept, beginning in a very small way.

Far right: *Dugald Drummond's private inspection saloon* The Bug. ADRIAN KNOWLES COLLECTION

Right: *London Brighton & South Coast Railway Locomotive Superintendent William Stroudley's inspection saloon converted from a 'Terrier' 0-6-0T was not a railmotor per se, but like* The Bug, *had some of their characteristics.* ADRIAN KNOWLES COLLECTION

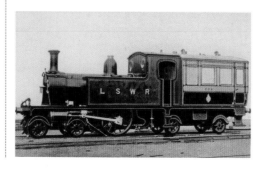

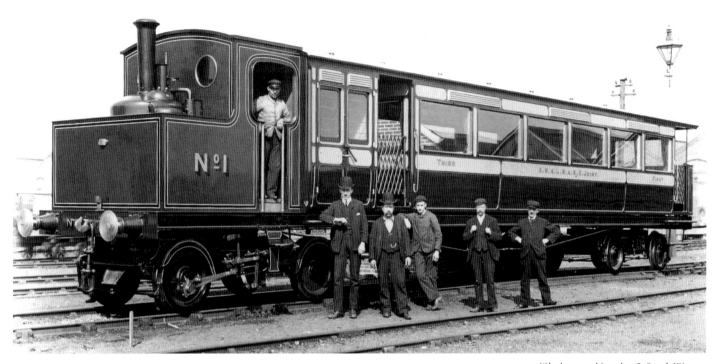

The borrowed London & South Western Railway No. 1 which sparked off the Edwardian railmotor revolution.
ADRIAN KNOWLES COLLECTION

For the 1.2 mile-branch from Fratton to East Southsea, run jointly with the London, Brighton & South Coast Railway, and on which the elimination of run-round times would certainly prove cost effective, he ordered the construction of an eight-wheeled bogie car, No. 1.

What was basically a combined engine and carriage was 56ft long with two cylinders 7in by 10in, a small vertical boiler operating at 150lb/sq in and 33in diameter wheels. The motor bogie was built at Nine Elms Works and the coach body at Eastleigh Carriage Works.

The idea of attaching an engine to a carriage was by then new to neither railways nor Drummond. In 1899, he ordered the building of a curious 4-2-4T comprising a locomotive and integral coach section built at Nine Elms Works as his private saloon. Nicknamed *The Bug*, and somewhat resembling the Great Southern & Western Railway's carriage engines, he used it to make random inspections right across the system – where Drummond's unexpected appearance could be a fearsome experience for railwaymen – as well as commuting from his home in Surbiton to Nine Elms, a practice that he continued when the LSWR works was moved to Eastleigh in 1908.

Hand-coloured picture of No. 1, the first steam railmotor built by the GWR. GWS

No. 1, one of the first two GWR railmotors which proved a dazzling success on the Golden Valley line. GWS

After Drummond's death in 1912, *The Bug* was little used, and was stored out of use at Eastleigh from 1916. It was returned to service briefly in 1932 to take small parties of visitors around the new Southampton Docks extensions before being finally withdrawn in 1940. The locomotive portion was scrapped but the carriage section survived for quite some time as the works foreman's office!

Before Drummond's first steam railmotor proper entered service on the south coast on 1 June 1903, however, the GWR asked to borrow it, for trials on the main line through the Golden Valley between Stroud and Chalford, the route of the later 'Cheltenham Flyer.'

Here, the GWR wanted to find an appealing alternative to local plans for a light railway or electric tramway running in parallel to its main line, a scheme proposed because of local dissatisfaction with the train service.

The interior of GWR steam railmotor No. 1. GWS

Alarm at GWR headquarters had already been sounded by the 75 per cent drop in passenger numbers between Camborne and Redruth in Cornwall after an electric street tramway linking the mining towns was opened. It was feared that such tramways would jeopardise the viability of several routes. A public-pleasing alternative to them had to be quickly found.

The GWR's general manager Sir Joseph Wilkinson, had already recommended in April 1903 that two steam railmotors should be built to a design by Chief Mechanical Engineer George Jackson Churchward for the Golden Valley line, as part of an experiment to see if they could boost the uptake of rural services, with extra stopping places provided. The Golden Valley, at that time a heavily-industrialised part of the Cotswolds with an economy based around woollen mills, would provide a perfect testbed, with a huge potential catchment area of workers travelling to and from factories in a comparatively narrow corridor.

The order for the railmotors was duly placed in May that year, while on 7 May, the LSWR railmotor ran to Swindon, via Addison Road at Kensington. On 10 May, Churchward himself ran this railmotor up and down between Stroud and Chalford and, clearly impressed, returned to Swindon to continue with his own designs.

Not only was Churchward impressed by the removal of the need to run round, but the railmotor was economical to operate and could be used on lightly-used lines. Furthermore, it could stop at unmanned halts which would be far too short for a conventional train comprising a locomotive and carriages.

Therefore GWR gained exemptions from the Board of Trade for minimalist halts which would be served by the railmotors. These lacked raised platforms, shelters and signals:

retractable steps on the coach body would allow the passengers to board and alight.

The first intermediate stopping places on the Golden Valley route were designated as St Mary's Crossing, Ham Mill Crossing and Cairns Cross, between Stroud and Stonehouse.

Interestingly, while the automobile industry was in its infancy, the steam railmotors were referred to as 'motor car trains' at this period.

The first two GWR steam railmotors, appropriately numbered 1 and 2, and each seating 52 passengers, entered service over the 7 miles between Stonehouse and Chalford on 12 October 1903, when new rail-level platforms accessible only by these vehicles were opened at Ebley Crossing, Downfield Crossing, Ham Mill Crossing and St Mary's Crossing.

Nos. 1 and 2 were built to Diagram A1 at a cost of £1,738 12s each. They were 57ft 0¼in long, 8ft 6¾in wide and 12ft 6in high from the rail to the roof.

Specifications for GWR steam railmotor No. 2. GWS

The power unit and driving cab were contained in a separate compartment, which included the boiler, firebox and coal bunker.

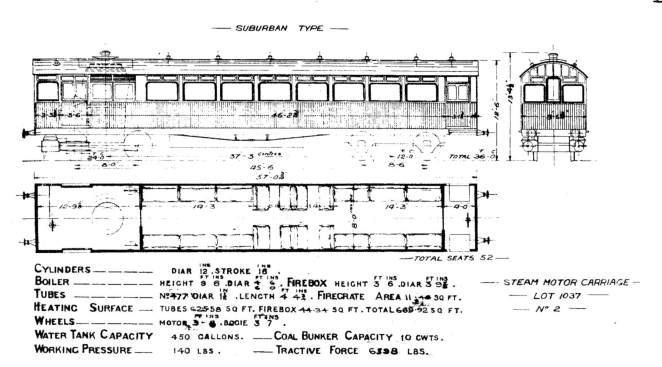

The boiler on No. 1 was said to produce 180lbs/sq in and a tractive effort of 8,483lbs.

Both power bogies had 3ft 8in driving wheels when built, although both vehicles underwent many modifications during the course of their working lives. The water tank held 450 gallons and was located under the coach between the frames.

Both cars had wooden bodies, with the upper exterior panelling being Honduras mahogany and the lower half matchboarding, fixed to an oak frame.

Interior lighting was provided by gas lamps. Passengers rode in a large open single-class saloon accessed through the driving vestibule at the trailing end, but the crew could access the saloon through a sliding door.

Crew members at either end could communicate through battery-powered electrical bells, while a cord running in a tube through the passenger compartment operated the whistle: the tube was fitted with leather straps for standing passengers to grasp.

The railmotor services ran from Mondays to Saturdays, running each hour from 8am to 9pm from Chalford to Stonehouse and on the half hours in the opposite direction, with extra runs on Fridays and Saturdays. The extra paths for the railmotors on this route became available through the opening of the South Wales and Bristol direct Line from Wootton Bassett to Patchway, relieving the Swindon-Gloucester line of through traffic to South Wales.

THE RAILMOTOR REVOLUTION STARTS

The Golden Valley railmotors were a overnight success, as the local population immediately took them to their hearts. Before their introduction, around 1300 passengers a week travelled between the stations that they served.

Possibly boosted somewhat by the novelty value, 2,500 passengers were carried on the first day of railmotor operation alone, and nearly 12,000 in the first week. On the Saturday, the demand for places was so great that the two cars had to be coupled together, making what would become known in those early days as a "double unit".

A report on the Chalford and Stonehouse service presented to the GWR Traffic Committee in January 1904 said: "The carryings by the motor cars and the local passenger trains average 1,354 passengers per day and 474,000 per annum. Prior to the introduction of the cars the carryings were 194 per day and 68,000 per annum. This gives an increase of 597 per cent."

Any business would be way over the moon at sudden booms in trade of that magnitude, and it went without saying that GWR headquarters at Paddington was at least impressed, and in all reality was more likely ecstatic beyond words. It was as if a transport concept which had been screaming to be let out of the bag for half a century had finally got its way.

The purpose of a railway company is not necessarily to convey people and goods from one point to another, but to make a profit in doing so. Serendipity – the action of discovery by chance – saw a bespoke solution to a local problem lift the lid off a treasure chest of untapped railway potential.

The towering triumph of the two railmotors saw the rival tramway scheme disappear without trace, and the GWR immediately and understandably viewed the concept as heralding a lucrative future for branch lines, both in sparsely-populated rural locations and in urban areas, where the emergence of street trams meant that the railway had to fight harder for its passengers than ever before.

The Chalford experiment sparked off a railway revolution, one which would impinge on many areas not just of the GWR empire but the national network as a whole within a few years. It proved a point too often forgotten in the twentieth century: repackage rail services so that they

The Cotswold village of Chalford, where British railway history changed forever thanks to the debut of the first two GWR railmotors. GWS

cater for the immediate needs of the local population – and the customers will respond.

Watching the success of the Golden Valley operation, other railway companies too began muscling in on the act, but it was the GWR that invested most heavily in the concept, and ended up with the biggest steam railmotor fleet of them all.

THE GWR RAILMOTOR FLEET

In the wake of the phenomenal success of the first two railmotors in the Golden Valley, orders were quickly placed by the GWR for a further 44 which were completed between 1904 and 1905.

By 1908, when production stopped, there were 99 carriage units, but 112 power units, the reason being that power units could be exchanged during maintenance.

On Sunday 1 May 1904, two railmotor services were launched in west London, the first between Southall and Westbourne Park, over the new Acton and Northolt line. Four new railmotor halts were provided, at North Acton, Twyford Abbey, Perivale (soon enlarged because of its huge popularity) and Castle Bar Park. The second was on the sparsely-used Southall to Brentford branch. At Southall, a corrugated iron shed for housing three railmotors was built. On 1 July that year, another service was launched, between Park Royal, the Greenford loop and Acton.

On 1 November 1905, a railmotor service especially for Post Office staff was launched between Southall and Paddington.

Another major success story for the railmotors was Plymouth, where they provided a frequent service competing against the city's new electric tramway, as well as rival LSWR lines. Suburban railmotor services between Saltash, Plymouth (Millbay) and Plympton, and

No. 93, sole surviving GWR steam railmotor, seen in Edwardian times on the Clevedon branch, where, ironically, the pioneer example, the Fairfield *steam carriage, may have run half a century before.*
H.C. CASSERLEY

GWR steam railmotor No. 2 is seen at Ebley Crossing Halt, which was opened on 12 October 1903 on what is now the Golden Valley line between Stroud and Stonehouse. GWS

between Plymouth and the rural backwater of Yealmpton, were introduced on 1 June 1904, with new halts being built at Laira, Lipson Vale, Wingfield Villas, Ford and St Budeaux.

In the first 12 days of the Plymouth-Saltash railmotor service, passenger numbers soared by 25,339 with receipts rising by nearly three quarters. On the Yealmpton branch, numbers increased by a far more modest 1,148 with receipts up 10 %. In 1905, the most productive of all the GWR railmotor services anywhere was the Sunday Plymouth to Tavistock.

Continuing Plymouth's great seafaring tradition, a railmotor stop, Defiance Halt, was built by sailors nearly a mile west of Saltash, to serve the Torpedo Instruction Ship HMS *Defiance*. It opened in March 1905, but was quickly rendered obsolete, as the GWR had decided to build a deviation between St Germans and Saltash, with a replacement Defiance Platform opening on it in May the following year.

From their Plymouth base, steam railmotors were also trialled at Penzance, and Newton Abbot. On Saturday 1 October 1904, railmotors took over services on the Totnes to Ashburton line, part of which nowadays forms the South Devon Railway.

In North Wales, railmotors appeared on the Ruabon to Dolgellau route from 1 July 1904, and on the lines from Wrexham to Rhos and to Coed Porth from 1 October that year.

In the Midlands, railmotor services between Stratford-upon-Avon, Honeybourne and Cheltenham were progressively introduced from 24 October 1904, and by 1 August 1906, all local service between the latter two was in the hands of railmotors.

Railmotors began operating between Kidderminster, Bewdley, Stourport and Hartlebury on 2 January 1905, with a new halt being built at Foley Park, on the part of the route which now forms the southern section of the Severn Valley Railway.

Across the GWR network, railmotor services became very popular and within a few years, housing estates sprang up near to the halts. Demand for seats at peak periods was so high that trailer cars were attached, with a driving compartment at the end of the trailer car fitted with duplicate controls. The Steam Multiple Unit had arrived!

Railmotors allowed the Great Western Railway to provide additional services economically between normal passenger trains, with extra intermediate stopping places. This allowed and indeed enticed more people to travel on the routes concerned and at the outset greatly boosted revenue.

There were basically five different types of GWR railmotor. Nos 1 and 2 were the flat-ended prototypes introduced to the Golden Valley line, Nos 3-14 were matchboarded carriages, Nos. 15 and 16 were built by Kerr Stuart to their own design, Nos. 17-28 were a

Calling at Dawlish is GWR steam railmotor No. 38, more than half a century after Brunel's atmospheric railway serving the South Devon resort gave way to steam haulage. Atmospheric propulsion was quickly forgotten, but the railmotor left a far-reaching legacy. GWS

Railmotor No.97 on the GWR Teign Valley line between Exeter and Heathfield. GWS

Above: *The boiler of brand new steam railmotor No. 73 being lifted into the coach body at the Gloucester Railway Carriage & Wagon works in 1906. This is clearly a photo posed for the camera as no ashpan is fitted to the boiler.* GWS

No. 17, the first in a second series of 12 matchboarded railmotors. GWS

Above left: *Steam railmotor No. 85 near Pangbourne on the GWR's Reading to Oxford line.* GWS

Above right: *Railmotor No. 72 calls at St Agnes on the Newquay to Chacewater line in Cornwall.* GWS

Railmotors Nos. 40 and 93 on shed, possibly at Stourbridge, although the exact location is unclear. GWS

In this photograph, taken around 1919 to record the sinking of foundations for the extension to the famous 'A' Erecting Shop at Swindon Works, three railmotors can be seen. Nos. 77 and 80 are from the Gloucester RC&W batch, while No. 16 is one of the non-standard Kerr Stuart cars. All are in crimson lake livery. A vertical railmotor boiler stands in front of No. 77. GWS second type of matchboarded carriages and Nos. 29-99 were the standard GWR type, of which No. 93 is a classic example.

The first 16 steam railmotors were built for passenger use only, and were referred to as the 'suburban' type. However, from No. 17 onwards, each had small luggage compartment for carrying small items, and were referred to as 'branch' types.

A total of 14 of the GWR steam railmotors were built by Kerr Stuart of Stoke-on-Trent and eight by the Gloucester Carriage & Wagon Company, but the remainder were all Swindon products, mostly with 12in by 16in cylinders and 48in driving wheels. The Kerr Stuart types were 70ft long, with Nos. 61-72 built to a GWR design, while the Gloucester ones, Nos. 73-80 were 59ft 6in long, and also of Swindon design. All 22 were the branch type.

The use of steam railmotors by the GWR peaked around 1913, when they ran in excess of two million miles.

Hand-tinted contemporary postcard of railmotor No. 45 at Penzance, the westernmost extremity of the GWR empire. ROBIN JONES COLLECTION

Cutting edge city transport technology a century ago: a GWR steam railmotor on Paddington suburban duties. GWS

Railmotor No. 35 and station staff at Stourport-on-Severn on the Severn Valley line. GWS

GWR steam railmotor No. 9 at Stanley Bridge Halte on the Calne branch. Complete with GWR pagoda, the halt was opened in 1905 especially for the railmotor service. The 'e' in Halte, a continental-style term invented for railmotor stops, was later dropped throughout the GWR system. GWS

It was rare to see steam railmotor engine units outside the coach body. This pair is awaiting overhaul at Swindon Works. GWS

THE HARES AND THE TORTOISES

At the same time as Churchward was designing his first railmotors, a batch of ten locomotives, the 3700 or City class 4-4-0s were outshopped from Swindon in May 1903. A year later, one of them, No. 3440 *City of Truro*, was timed at a speed of 102.3mph by recorder Charles Rous-Marten, a writer for *The Railway Magazine*, as it hauled the 'Ocean Mails' special from Plymouth to Paddington while descending Wellington Bank on 9 May 1904.

   While two local Plymouth newspapers reported the next day that the train had reached

Unofficial steam recordbreaker No. 3440 City of Truro *heading a modern-day 'Scarborough Spa Express'.* NRM

between 99 and 100mph on Wellington Bank, based on the stopwatch timings of postal worker William Kennedy, who was also on the train, the GWR, mindful of the fact that passengers were suspicious of high speeds and feared crashes, allowed only the overall timings to be published.

Rous-Marten did not publish the alleged maximum speed for another year, and even then he steered clear of naming the railway company or the engine concerned.

However, before he died in 1908, he revealed that it was *City of Truro*. Yet it was not until 1922, when railway companies were trying to promote the speed of their trains, that the GWR confirmed Rous-Marten's report and its timings, which have ever since been the subject of controversy, although he has in recent times been supported by computer simulations of the run.

Hide it as they might, the GWR had produced a world beater as far as steam traction was concerned, although No. 3440 could not claim to be the fastest vehicle of any type, as 126mph had been recorded on an experimental electric railway near Berlin in 1903.

It would not be until November 1934 that LNER Pacific No. 4412 *Flying Scotsman* would officially break the 100mph barrier on the East Coast Main Line, four years before streamlined

A4 Pacific No. 4468 *Mallard* set the still-unbeaten official world railway steam speed record of 126mph.

Yet while chief mechanical engineers were competing against each other to see who could produce the most powerful and fastest railway locomotive, the humble and barely illustrious railmotor was blazing the real trail to the future, in which multiple-unit trains, not big glamorous locomotives, form the backbone of today's modern rail network.

THE RAILMOTOR BANDWAGON ROLLS

Have instant commercial success with a new product, whether it be microwave ovens, video records and digital cameras, and within months, competitors will follow suit. The same is true for the railmotor concept.

After the lukewarm reception to the Adams pioneers on the mid nineteenth-century, few in Victorian times would have predicted such a rip-roaring success to the Edwardian railmotors.

The Taff Vale Railway had the second biggest steam railmotor fleet after the GWR. Pictured is No. 15 with its crew. GWS

Other companies had in early Edwardian times identified the same needs on rural and suburban lines as the GWR, and if they had not already been considering the railmotor concept, they were quick to take it up once they saw the astonishing results from the early GWR services.

Basically, there were two distinct types of steam railmotor. The first was the type we have seen in action on the GWR, effectively a coach body with a steam locomotive built into it, and usually powered by a vertical boiler. The second type had an 0-4-0 steam locomotive attached to a coach body, which acted like a trailer minus the couplings.

Outside the GWR, the greatest number of railmotors in these formative years was on the Lancashire & Yorkshire Railway, which built 18 of the second type between 1905-11 onwards. One of them formed the 'Altcar Bob' service introduced in July 1906 on the Barton branch of the Liverpool, Southport and Preston Junction Railway. The name came from the fact that trains initially terminated Altcar and Hillhouse, although nobody now knows who or what 'Bob' was.

The service ceased when the line closed to passengers on 26 September

1938, with the last L&Y railmotor withdrawn by British Railways in 1948.

After the L&Y came the Taff Vale Railway, which built 18 steam railmotors, the first entering service just two months after those of the GWR's Golden Valley route.

Taff Vale general manager Ammon Beasley feared competition from a proposed electric tramway between Cardiff and Penarth, and asked locomotive engineer Hurry Riches to look at the possibility of electrifying the company's own Penarth line, but that was deemed non viable. Then battery-electric and petrol-electric railcars were considered, and Vincent Raven's North Eastern Railway autocars (see following chapter) were inspected. Nothing came of this, and by June 1903, Riches had inspected the LSWR steam railmotor and had recommended that the Taff Vale should build one of its own.

Railmotor No. 1 was the only one built in the Taff Vale's own works at Cardiff, and incidentally, also the last locomotive that it constructed. The steam locomotive part of this articulated vehicle was erected in the company's West Yard at Cardiff Docks and the coach body was built at its Cathays carriage works.

After trials, the railmotor, which was of the type which had the engine attached to the body rather than concealed inside, entered experimental service between Cardiff and Cadoxton in December 1903. Daily operations between Cardiff and Penarth began on the 21st of that month. By February, figures showed that the running costs of the steam railmotor on the route were just a third of those of a 'normal' train.

It had a first and a third class compartment.

Official Gloucester Railway Carriage & Wagon photograph of one of the Cardiff Railway steam railmotors.
GWS

The Port Talbot Railway's one and only steam railmotor. GWS

No. 1 so impressed Riches and the Taff Vale board that six more railmotors broadly similar in design were ordered in February 1904 from the Avonside Engine Company of Bristol and Bristol Wagon & Carriage Ltd. They first entered service between Pontypridd and Nelson on 10 October 1904, and a week later, began running between Ynysybwl and Abercynon. A local Aberdare service started on 26 November 1904.

Six more cars, Nos. 8-13, were ordered in October 1904, from Kerr Stuart, with Bristol Wagon & Carriage Ltd. again providing the bodywork. These were third class only, but thoughtfully had separate compartments for ladies and non-smokers.

Three more along with two extra engines, Nos 14-18, were ordered from Manning Wardle of Leeds in September 1905, with Brush Electrical Engineering of Loughborough supplying the carriage bogies. Composites, they accommodated 16 first class and 57 third class passengers, the former divided into smoking and non-smoking areas.

The LSWR continued down the railmotor route by building a second car for the Southsea line, again in conjunction with the LBSCR, followed by two more in the company's own right, and also numbered 1 and 2. Built to order H12, and of the locomotive-attached-to-carriage type, these entered service on the Basingstoke to Alton line in May and June 1904, and unlike the pioneer GWR railmotors, No. 2 was converted to electric lighting.

Seven more, Nos 3-9, were ordered by the LSWR in May 1905. These were built to order H13 and were somewhat of a retrograde step in having interior gas as opposed to the electric lighting present in No. 2. Delivered between December 1905 and February 1906, another pair, Nos 10 and 11, followed a month later. Finally, four more LSWR railmotors were built, two to order A14, Nos. 12 and 13, in May 1906, and two to order B14, in June that year.

The Great Northern Railway had six articulated (as opposed to the far more prevalent rigid design) railmotors designed by Chief Locomotive Superintendent Henry Alfred Ivatt and built in 1905/6, again of the tank engine stapled to carriage type.

Referred to as 'motor coaches', the six vehicles were built in three batches of two. Each batch was constructed by a different manufacturer and had distinctive outlines.

Nos. 1 and 2 were built at Doncaster in 1905, and incidentally, were the first examples of Nigel Gresley's elliptical-roof coaching stock. The next pair, Nos. 5 and 6, were built by Kitson & Co. in December 1905 with the coachwork manufactured by Birmingham Carriage & Wagon Works.

Nos. 7 and 8 were built in February 1906 by Avonside in Bristol, with, as with some of the

Belfast & County Down railmotor No. 3 at Holywood. DCDR

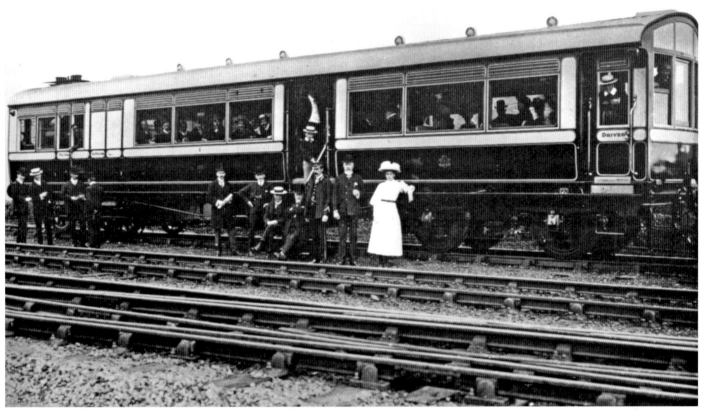

Railway staff and passengers pose outside a LNWR steam railmotor. GWS

Taff Vale railmotors, the coachwork supplied by Bristol Carriage & Wagon works.

All six had vacuum brakes, and were capable of hauling trailers. At least three older carriages were converted into trailers for them.

At first it was planned to operate them across the entire GNR system, but they were only used between Louth and Grimsby, Hitchin and Baldock, Finchley and Edgware, and on the Chickenley Heath branch. They had all been taken out of service by 1917, but resuscitated by the LNER in 1924, despite the fact that many area managers expressed disdain for them. They were used on a new passenger service between Hitchin and Hertford North between June and November 1924, but were finally withdrawn in 1925/6.

The LBSCR bought two from Beyer Peacock in 1905, with the Preston-based Electric Railway and Tramway Carriage Works building the bodies. Not a success, they ended up in

A poster advertising London Brighton & South Coast Railway steam railmotor services. ADRIAN KNOWLES COLLECTION

Trinidad where the carriage body from one was turned into a saloon for the Governor.

The London & North Western Railway built six rigid 57ft steam railmotors during 1905/6, and a 60ft one in 1901.

The North Staffordshire Railway introduced three Beyer Peacock 40-seater railmotors in 1905. They ran on several rural routes including today's Churnet Valley Railway until their withdrawal in 1922.

Other British companies that ran railmotors in the Edwardian era included the Great Central Railway (three), the Alexandra (Newport & South Wales) Dock & Railway Company (two), the Barry Railway (two), Furness Railway (two), the Rhymney Railway (two), the Cardiff Railway (two) and the Port Talbot Railway (one).

The first Edwardian railmotor in Ireland was built by the GSWR at Inchicore in 1904. Designed by R. Coey, the company's Chief Mechanical Engineer for use on the 5¾-mile Gould's Cross to Cashel branch, it was based on Drummond's pioneer LSWR railmotor.

However, it often broke down, and was not powerful enough to haul a trailer. It was withdrawn in 1912, ending the GSWR's flirtations with the railmotor concept.

As with the GWR and the Golden Valley line, in 1904 the Belfast & County Down Railway was threatened with tramway competition and ordered two steam railmotors to boost its Holywood suburban service. Kitson provided the power units and the Metropolitan Railway Carriage & Wagon Co. the coach section.

They proved popular and a third followed in 1906, but lack of maintenance during World War One left them worn out by 1918, and they were converted to auto-trailers.

The Midland Railway (Northern Counties Committee) had two steam railmotors built at Derby in 1905, but were withdrawn by 1913.

The biggest operator of railmotors in Ireland was the Great Northern Railway (Ireland) which bought three enclosed vertical-boilered types in 1905 from the North British Locomotive Co. of Glasgow and four from Manning Wardle the following year. The power units were similar to those fitted to the GWR railmotors.

All seven were withdrawn in 1913 and converted into coaches.

In August 1906, the Dublin, Wicklow & Wexford Railway bought two railmotors from Manning Wardle for a new service between Bray and Greystones south of Dublin. After withdrawal as railmotors, the locomotive sections became shunting locomotives, which were scrapped in 1931.

LIFE ON THE RAILMOTORS

While the GWR railmotors emerged as the surprise success of the Edwardian era, it was not all plain sailing.

On the Golden Valley line, the GWR had planned to charge a fare of halfpenny a mile, with a minimum fare of a penny. The intermediate stopping places would be unstaffed, with the tickets issued by conductors who would also act as deputy drivers.

However, this service did not achieve the half-hourly schedule that the Swindon hierarchy had envisaged.

The guards objected to issuing tickets as they said that the machines they were given were too cumbersome. Automatic ticket machines sited on the halt platforms were considered, but the GWR decided that they were too costly at £100 each.

Despite the popularity of the railmotors, the fare structure had not been worked out as well as it might have been. Brimscombe to Ham Mill and Ham Mill to Stroud both cost a penny, but Brimscombe to Stroud cost threepence – whereas the rival bus cost just twopence.

Few people today can tell us about life on the railmotors, both from a staff and passenger point of view.

The Great Western Society tracked down Wolverhampton railmotor fireman Walther Cottam, who related his memories to member Mike Lewis.

He described shovelling coal on a railmotor from a wheelbarrow and said that the storage capacity of the bunker to be about as much use as a shelf! The water tank was so small that it needed to be filled at the end of the Wolverhampton to Stourbridge via Wombourne route.

Despite GWR advice about good firing practice, such as firing only when the

A clue to the working conditions on the steam railmotors is given in many photographs which show all the doors and windows of the engine compartment wide open. On a hot day it must have been quite arduous for the fireman. GWS

regulator was open to avoid unnecessary smoke, this would have been a disaster if applied on the railmotors, said Walter. The deep circular firebox had a firehole positioned immediately below the tubeplate, and opening the door would send cold secondary air straight across it and up the vertical tubes. Therefore, at every station stop, the fireman would frantically recharge the firebox to recover lost ground in the steam and water before the railmotor took off again.

One day, just after departure, Walter heard a hiss of steam on top of the boiler repeated several times. Suddenly an enormous blast of steam filled the cab roof – because the whistle pillar had snapped clean off!

William Harbour, the son of a GWR goods guard, was born in Clevedon in 1920 regularly travelled by railmotor on the branch from Yatton as a schoolboy. It was on the branch where Adams' *Fairfield* carriage had run in broad gauge days that he had his first experience of the inside of the railmotor's cab.

He said: "Once or twice, when the driver and fireman were waiting for the next run from Clevedon I was allowed to step up into the cab – where you could walk right round the back of the boiler. Of course, it was a rather low-pressure boiler so they were not built for speed; in fact, they were limited to 45 miles an hour. But there was not much room in the cab; the railmotor had a very short wheelbase and being short of space, it was able to carry only relatively limited amounts of coal.

"I do recall that when the whistle was blown it was very different to the distinctive, clear-cut sound associated with regular Great Western trains. It was more of a strangulated, watery kind of whistle.

One of the serious limitations of steam railmotors was their lack of power for hauling additional vehicles when traffic demanded it. One trailer and perhaps a horsebox or van was usually the maximum load, and even that could prove a struggle on lines with heavier gradients. This railmotor and trailer pairing is seen at Gerrards Cross in about 1914. GWS

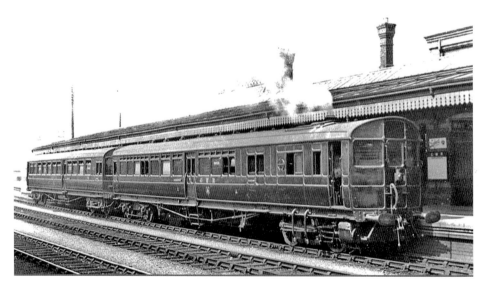

"What I remember most about my rail journeys as a youngster in the railmotors was the shuffling nature of the things. I suppose that would be down to the low-pressure boiler. The jerking movement meant that it was not really a very comfortable ride.

"I have to admit I did rather despise the things as a child! If I remember rightly they used to jerk quite a bit when they pulled away – and the jerking became even more pronounced after the sharp turn out of Yatton. It was a very uneven motion."

CHAPTER THREE
THE NEXT STEP:
THE PETROL-ELECTRIC AUTOCAR

MORE THAN HALF A century after the concept was first demonstrated, the self-propelled all-in-one rail vehicle in the form of the steam railmotor caught on big time, but as we have seen, their inherent disadvantages prompted their demise within three decades.

Yet what if the dirty, grimy, maintenance-intensive steam locomotive component in its cramped confines could be dispensed with, and replaced with a cleaner and more efficient type of self-propelled traction that would be easier both to operate and service?

By the turn of the century, the influence of Magnus Volk had spread far and wide, with the emergence of both electric street trams and electric railways. The City & South London Railway became the world's first electric underground line when it opened on 18 December 1890. The first section of the Liverpool Overhead Railway opened in 1893, the Mersey

Autocar No. 3170 and a trailer in NER service. AUTOCAR TRUST

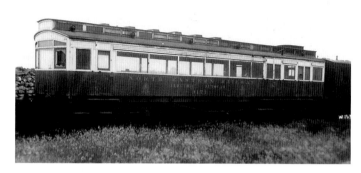

Above left: *One of the petrol-electric autocars inside York station.*
AUTOCAR TRUST

Above right: *NER autocar No. 3171, the one which did not survive.*
PETER MIDDLETON

Railway was electrified in 1903, the Metropolitan railway 'Inner Circle' in 1905 and the Midland Railway's Morecambe-Heysham line in 1908.

Electrification offered the advantage of rapid acceleration, ideal for urban and suburban lines, which had many stops over a short distance and needed to run intensive timetables, but because of the huge initial outlay, the main railway companies did not consider it an economically viable replacement for steam over their entire networks.

Drawing on experiments with tram technology, the Taff Vale Railway looked at the possibility of using battery-electric railcars and also a petrol-electric railcar for a lightly-used rural route, but nothing came of it. The GWR actually produced a diagram of a petrol-engined railcar in February 1903, before any of the company's steam railmotors got off the drawing board, and before the company began using petrol road buses on its route from Helston to Lizard Town in August that year, both as a feeder to their train services, and as a cheaper alternative to building new lines in sparsely-populated rural areas.

The North Eastern Railway went one better, and in terms of technological evolution, eclipsed everyone else. In 1903, while Churchward was testing his borrowed LSWR railcar, the NER made history by taking the steam railmotor concept to the next stage before it had managed to get off the ground, and before the GWR had built its first pair for the Golden Valley line.

In May that year, the NER outshopped a pair of 'autocars'. They were the first internal combustion engined self-propelled passenger-carrying rail vehicles in the world, and through them, the steam railmotor concept would evolve into the diesel railcar of the 1930s and beyond to the high-speed multiple units of today's railways.

The NER's Assistant Chief Mechanical Engineer Vincent Raven was convinced about the

Autocar No. 3170 leaving Scarborough. AUTOCAR TRUST

The interior of the petrol-electric autocars. AUTOCAR TRUST

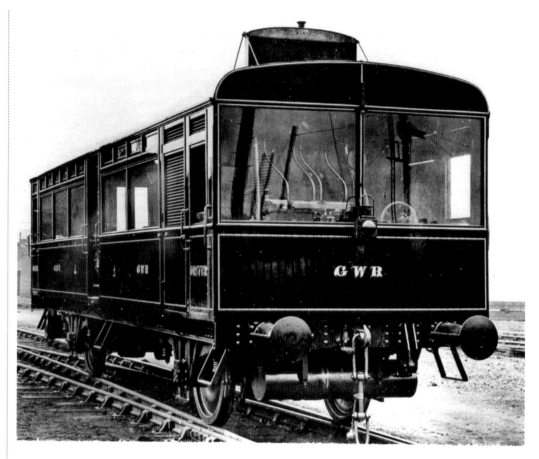

The GWR's petrol-electric vehicle failed to have anything like the same impact as steam railmotors. GWS

advantages of electric traction, especially with regard to the hill climbing ability of the early street trams that he studied.

Raven drew up a design for his autocars incorporating electrical technology, but instead of picking up the current from overhead lines in tram fashion, he eliminated the need for expensive wires and masts by installing a power plant within the vehicle instead. In other words, his autocar design was a steam railmotor minus the steam engine but with an 85hp Napier petrol engine powering a dynamo which supplied 550V to two 55hp electric motors, which drove the axles of the power bogie via gears.

The autocars were similar in appearance to the Tyneside electric stock that was being built at the same time, with matchboard sides, large windows, and a clerestory roof. The big difference was that the autocars could go anywhere, while the Tyneside trains were limited to electrified routes.

Back in 1903, the motor car was still very much in its embryonic stages and petrol engines were still comparatively primitive. Adequate diesel engines were not developed until the mid 1930s.

The power bogie, petrol engine and generator were all positioned at the front, along with the main driving controls. A smaller driving compartment was situated at the rear.

Reversible seats on both sides of a central gangway provided seating for 52 passengers, who accessed the saloon through side doors located at both ends. Unlike the steam railmotors of the day which used interior gas lighting, electric lighting was provided.

Another first for the NER autocars, numbered 3170 and 3171, was that they were fitted with electric track brakes, similar to those used on tramcars. Each autocar was also fitted with a hand screw brake and a Westinghouse air brake.

The original petrol engines proved problematical during tests, and they were replaced with Wolseley horizontally-opposed 85hp four-cylinder engines. Around the same time the 30-gallon petrol tanks were replaced with 70 gallon tanks.

The pair entered service in August 1904.

Just as the GWR built its first two steam railmotors to see off a rival electric tramway

Passengers queuing to board the petrol-electric autocar at Scarborough.
AUTOCAR TRUST

51

Just like GWR steam railmotor No. 93, the NER petrol-electric autocars were originally but briefly painted in crimson lake livery.
AUTOCAR TRUST

scheme, at first one of the NER railcars entered traffic between West Hartlepool and Hartlepool stations in direct competition with electric street trams, and showed it could complete the journey in half the time of the rival service.

The other replaced steam on the Scarborough to Filey route.

One of them replaced steam push-pull trains for around six months on the Billingham-Port Clarence line in 1904/5.

In 1908, they were allocated to work passenger services on the Selby-Cawood branch. A purpose-built shed was erected to house them at Selby in early 1913.

The pair were initially painted using the standard NER crimson lake coaching livery, but were soon repainted into red and cream.

In 1923, No. 3170 was fitted with a six-cylinder 225hp war surplus engine and a bigger dynamo, providing it with sufficient power to pull a single carriage and increasing passenger capacity, and was repainted in LNER teak livery with the number 3170Y. Reallocated to Harrogate Starbeck shed, it briefly ran return trips from there to Knaresborough, Ripon,

Pannal, Pateley Bridge and Wetherby, but was back at Selby by the end of the year.

The autocars fell out of favour in the twenties. One big criticism was that their weight of 35 tons 15 cwt was high for the relatively low power output. Also, there was the old problem of two 'one off' types of 'unusual' traction in a 'Big Four' company fleet dominated by steam. History, however, supports those who believe that the Raven autocars were decades ahead of their time.

No. 3171 was withdrawn on May 31 1930 and No. 3170Y in April 1931. The body of the latter was sold to a North Yorkshire landowner and fitted with a tin roof and veranda, became a holiday home at Keldholme near Kirkbymoorside on the North Yorkshire moors.

The LBSCR bought a pair of Dick Kerr petrol-driven four-wheel carriages in 1905, but were unsuccessful in service and became inspection vehicles for overhead conductors on electrified suburban lines.

The Great Western Railway did go ahead with a petrol-electric railcar, but eight years after the NER pair appeared. On 3 November 1910, the board appointed the British Thomson-

No. 3170 in LNER teak livery in 1923. AUTOCAR TRUST

Houston Company of Rugby to build a prototype light self-propelled vehicle.

Built in 1911, by the following year the 46-seater vehicle, No. 100, was undergoing trials on the Windsor branch, providing nine journeys a day to Slough and back.

Power was supplied by a 40hp Maudsley petrol engine coupled to a dynamo which supplied current to two motors on the axle. The dead weight per passenger was half that of a GWR steam railmotor with the same carrying capacity, with the result that less space was required for fuel. The maximum speed was 35mph, and the vehicle was fitted with a Westinghouse brake. Unusually, the radiator was positioned upright on the roof.

Predicting the modern railcar and minimalist branch line operation of today, only one man was needed to drive the car, although a conductor travelled at the opposite end, to attend to the engine if needed to do so.

At the time of the trials, the GWR had the option of buying the car, and apparently did so by 1913. Its first official allocation was to Slough in 1914, but during the winter of 1914/15 it went to Swindon Works for repairs and modifications.

It was reallocated to Wormwood Scrubs in January 1917, but by November that year it was back at Swindon and in 1918 moved to Wolverhampton.

The GWR did not order further examples. A report indicated that the engine suffered from overheating of the detachable valve seatings which impaired its performance.

It was sold to Lever Brothers of Port Sunlight on 20 October 1919, and used on the firm's internal system on Merseyside until 1923, when it was withdrawn. Around 1927 the body was sold off for use as a holiday home at Prestatyn.

Sam Fey, the general manager of the Great Central Railway, was sufficiently impressed by the performance of petrol-electric railcars in Europe to buy a 50-seater bogie version from the Westinghouse Electric & Manufacturing Company in Manchester in 1912. Although it had a similar capacity, it was shorter, lighter and more powerful than the NER autocars, fitted with a six-cylinder 90hp petrol engine at the front powering a 55kw generator which supplied a pair of 64hp traction motors in the rear bogie. Both the cooling radiator and engine silencer were fixed on the roof, exposing the radiator to severe frosts and necessitating its emptying every night during the winter.

After trials in the Manchester area, it ran press trips between Marylebone and South Harrow on 28 March 1912, and two years later was allocated to the Glossop branch. At the Grouping of 1923, the LNER retained the original GCR teak livery and numbered it 51709.

It was after World War One that road traffic became established as a serious threat to the railways, and No. 51709 was allocated to a new shuttle service between Macclesfield Central and Bollington launched in August 1921. Nicknamed the 'Bollington Bug', it ran the service until it was withdrawn on 6 July 1935 and replaced by a Sentinel steam railcar.

CHAPTER FOUR
THE DEMISE OF THE STEAM RAILMOTOR

MANY A RAILWAY HIERARCHY looked at the startling early returns from their railmotor services, some on branch lines where income had always been comparatively modest, and thought it was too good to be true. In the medium to longer term, they were proved right.

The levels of trade they brought to many local lines was beyond the operating companies' wildest dreams. Indeed, the railmotors boosted traffic to the point where they could not cope with demand, even with a trailer attached.

Passenger capacity was not the only fault; some companies found that because of the smaller steam engines built into them, their lightweight railmotors floundered when coupled to extra vehicles, or at best ran sluggishly.

As a result, longer trains pulled by more powerful conventional steam locomotives, even small tank engines, again became necessary, making the railmotors the victims of their own sensational success.

While an all-in-one vehicle may be easy to operate, by eliminating turntables and run-round routes, and shortening the time between arrival at a terminus and departure, they were notoriously difficult to service. The cramped space of the engine compartment in the types which are based around a carriage with a locomotive built into it made maintenance awkward.

Furthermore, they needed to be serviced in a workshop, and because the coach body had to go in as well as the engine, they took up valuable space which could have been used for maintaining other vehicles. If there was a problem with the engine, the coach was laid up too, reducing available passenger vehicles.

Major repairs often needed the boiler or the entire power

Ageing GWR tank engines of the 517 class were given a new lease of life by being fitted with auto gear that enabled them to work with up to four trailers. As well as increasing operational flexibility, this meant that the locomotive could be serviced separately from the coaches and an engine failure would not disable the whole train. This scene is at Newnham, c.1906, with the locomotive in chocolate livery to match the chocolate and cream trailers.
GREAT WESTERN TRUST

unit to be lifted out of the body. This was a complex and painstaking process involving specialist equipment.

The interiors including the passenger accommodation were difficult to keep clean owing to the close proximity of the boiler, and the fact that they had to be serviced in grimy smoke-filled workshops.

While reaping big dividends from the introduction of the railmotors, Swindon also saw these drawbacks unfolding, and acted accordingly. In 1904, while railmotor production was getting into full swing, the GWR began fitting small tank engines with auto-control gear, allowing them to be controlled not only from the locomotive cab but also from the far end of specially-adapted carriages with a driver's vestibule built into one end and also fitted with the gear.

The creation of what became known as auto-trains, allowing the train to be push-pull worked, was a sideways step which gave the railways of the day the best of both worlds. Effectively, an auto train may be considered as a railmotor with a detachable engine. You still had the advantages of the railmotor, but the locomotive could also be used for other purposes, such as freight haulage, when the passenger service was not operating.

In at least one case, the Edwardian steam railmotor concept had been found wanting within just two years of being built. Two railmotors were built in 1905 for the Great North of Scotland Railway to a Pickersgill design using Andrew Barclay & Sons engines with the boilers made by Cochran & Co. of Annan. It was the only time that the renowned patent Cochran vertical boilers, with the distinctive near-hemispherical firebox and a large smokebox door on the side, were used in railway locomotives. The 45-passenger coach section was built at Inverurie Works, and the engines at Kilmarnock. The railmotors, numbered 29 and 31, were run between Inverness and Aberdeen and were recorded as having reached 60mph, with an acceleration of 0- 30mph in 20 seconds.

However, overall they were judged unsuccessful, and lasted only two years as railmotors. The locomotive sections are believed to have been scrapped as early as 1907 with the coach sections converted to bogie saloon thirds. Similar fates were to befall most railmotors in the decades ahead, with the carriage sections 'recycled'.

The South Eastern & Chatham Railway had eight stylish and elegant railmotors built under Locomotive, Carriage and Wagon Superintendent Harry Wainwright from 1904 onwards, but found them to be underpowered for purpose. While most had been withdrawn by 1914, two running between Hastings and Rye until February 1920, the Southern Railway inherited all eight sets, scrapped the locomotives and turned the carriage portions into four two-coach sets, two for the Sheppey Light Railway and two for Isle of Wight push-pull services.

Indeed, towards the end of the Edwardian era, the SECR built its diminutive P class 0-4-0 tank engines intending them to supplement and replace railmotors on rural branch lines.

The P class was an updated version of the LBSCR 'Terriers', but their small size meant that they were only slightly more successful than the railmotors, and increasingly relegated to shunting duties, as shed and station pilots.

The GWR began withdrawing its steam railmotors in 1914. The state of emergency that was placed on Britain's railways during World War One led to a huge reduction in railmotor mileage, which failed to recover after hostilities ceased. In 1923, GWR railmotor mileage reached a postwar high, but was still less than a million miles and much lower than in its Edwardian heyday. Three railmotors had by then been sold off to other companies and 38 withdrawn.

Again, many GWR railmotor carriage sections were converted into auto-trailers for push-pull services. The luggage compartment was moved to the end of the motor compartment, the remaining part of which along with the original luggage compartment were converted to longitudinal seating for 30 passengers. The remainder of the as-built passenger accommodation was retained.

All GWR railmotors had been taken out of the company's service by 1935, with No. 76 the last to be converted to a trailer car.

Between 1921–37, Bradford's Nidd Valley Railway, the only corporation operated passenger light railway in Britain, ran one that it had bought from the GWR. Named *Hill* at the time of its withdrawal, it had outlived the other 98 in service.

In terms of the evolution of passenger trains, as well as the huge social implications of widening the accessibility of cheap local rail travel, the railmotor had still very much made its mark. The all-in-one concept had been shown to work, but the problem was now viewed as the integral steam engine. Yet what if a cleaner more efficient form of motive power could instead be installed?

Despite the promising results with early petrol-electric railcars, the major companies were clearly reticent to go down that route en masse in a world where steam remained supreme, and the diesel engine was still in its infancy as far as railways were concerned.

Swindon's ideas of self-contained self-propelled passenger vehicles were therefore shunted into a siding, but they did not go away.

INDIAN SUMMER: THE SENTINEL AND CLAYTON RAILCARS

While the GWR was rapidly turning to auto trains to replace its steam railmotors, the concept enjoyed a significant rejuvenation elsewhere in the country.

Manufacturers Sentinel and Clayton came up with new designs which boasted high-speed engines. Shrewsbury-based Sentinel built its first steam railcar in 1923 for the 3ft 6in gauge Jersey Railways & Tramways Ltd, with Cammell Laird of Nottingham supplying the carriage body. Sentinel eventually supplied four to the Jersey Railway, and a standard gauge one to the

Jersey Eastern Railway.

The firm exhibited a second railcar at the British Empire Exhibition in 1924, and it attracted more than a few admiring glances from none other than Sir Nigel Gresley, designer of the great A1/A3 and A4 Pacifics including *Flying Scotsman* and *Mallard*.

The London & North Eastern Railway, where Gresley was Chief Mechanical Engineer, was searching for vehicles that would be cheaper to operate than conventional steam trains but which could carry more passengers than the Raven petrol-electric autocars and similar vehicles under consideration.

Between 17 and 31 August 1924, the LNER borrowed a railcar from Sentinel for trials in the north east. The experiment, which involved trials over the steeply-graded Whitby to Pickering line, now the North Yorkshire Moors Railway, proved successful and led to the LNER honouring a prior agreement to ordered two lightweight railcars with larger boilers in December that year. Eventually, the LNER bought a total of 80 Sentinel railcars between 1925-32, supplying four of them to the Cheshire Lines Committee which it controlled.

Most of the Sentinel railcars had a single engine equipped with a vertical water tube boiler. The cylindrical boiler had an outer shell with an inner firebox, with coal fed through a chute at the top, onto the grate at the bottom of the firebox.

One big advantage over earlier railmotor types was that the firebox was designed to be comparatively easily removed without having to lift the boiler out. This was just as well, because it was found that the Sentinel cars needed frequent changes of fireboxes.

The 80 railcars were produced in a series of small batches, each of which had marked mechanical and visual differences.

Far left: *Clayton steam railcar No. 2101* Union: *delivered in July 1928, it lasted only until April 1936 in LNER traffic.* STEPHEN MIDDLETON COLLECTION

Left: *The rear end of Clayton railcar No. 289* Wellington. STEPHEN MIDDLETON COLLECTION

All of the Sentinel steam railcars were named after old stage coaches. Most of them carried a notice detailing information about the stage coach and offering a reward for further information.

The LNER also acquired 1930-built Sentinel railcar No. 44 from the Axholme Joint Railway, which it jointly ran with the London Midland & Scottish Railway, when it ceased passenger services in 1933.

The Sentinel railcars suffered from boiler maintenance problems, especially with the water feed arrangements, and the collection of sediment due to inaccessibility of the washout holes near the base of the boiler.

The drive chains were found to stretch over time, and frame movement due to a lack of stability inherent in the design led to engine alignments being out of sync. Rising maintenance costs and World War Two austerity measures resulted in the withdrawals of all the LNER sentinel railcars by 1948. Some of them had lasted but a decade in service.

The Southern Railway bought a Sentinel-Cammell steam railcar in June 1933 for use on the Devil's Dyke branch in East Sussex. While operationally successful, it did not have the capacity to meet the passenger demand on this short line.

After being transferred from the line in March 1936 and trialled elsewhere, it was withdrawn in 1940.

Clayton Wagons Ltd of Lincoln began building steam railcars in 1927, and over the next 12 months sold 11 to the LNER. Broadly similar to the Sentinel versions, a big visual difference was the separate coal bunker and water tank carried on the power bogie to the front of the coach body.

The engine units had two cylinders with piston valves, and drive was provided via a spur gear on the driving axle. The axles on the power bogie were at first connected with a coupling rod, although these were often removed because of complaints that it caused the vehicles to vibrate.

The first car, No. 41, was delivered in July 1927 on an experimental basis, running between Lincoln and Woodhall Junction, and took the name *Pilot* when it was renumbered two years

LNER Sentinel steam railcar Ebor, *delivered in March 1928 and withdrawn in September 1939.* STEPHEN MIDDLETON COLLECTION

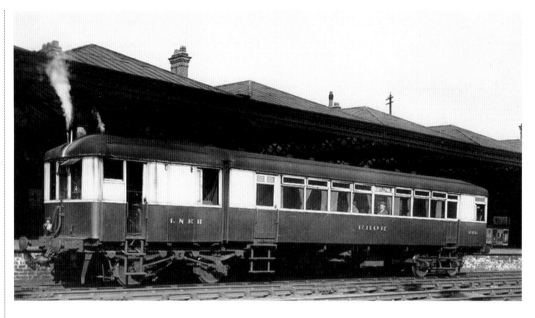

later as 2121. No. 41 was followed by the production batch of ten railcars, with seating capacity increased from 60 to 64 and the overall length a foot longer. Its first proper allocation saw it work York-Whitby-Scarborough-York circuit. Based at Heaton by six of the production batch, they operated services to Leamside, Morpeth, North Wylam, Prudhoe, and Blackhill. In the main, they were used on local short branch line runs. The final railcar was No. 2130, named *Bang Up*.

The LNER also bought eight four-wheeled 40-seater trailers from Clayton for use with the railcars.

Clayton went into liquidation in October 1929, leaving the LNER struggling to sources spare parts, and ended up having to make its own. The crankshafts were found to break often and the boilers were problematical, but one of the worst faults was the tendency to emit sparks, leading to spark arrestors having to be fitted.

The second Sentinel steam railcar delivered to the LNER was No. 13E, which was initially allocated to Cambridge. STEPHEN MIDDLETON COLLECTION

Railmotor *Rapid* became the first to be withdrawn in July 1932. Due to problems with reliability, in 1934 it was recommended that all the Heaton railcars should be withdrawn, although one of them, *Comet* was moved to Norwich that year, where three other cars were in service.

The last four were allocated to Lincoln, Doncaster, Norwich Lowestoft and Hitchin at various stages, and were withdrawn between April 1936 and February 1937.

One LNWR steam railmotor lasted in service until 1948. While the other six had been withdrawn by 1931, that year LMS No. 10697 was despatched to work the Moffat branch on the Calendonian Railway system.

In Ireland, the Great Southern Railway introduced four Sentinel steam railcars in late 1927 and used them until the 1940s. It also bought six steam railcars in 1928 from Clayton which were broadly identical to those in LNER service, but they were unsuccessful and were withdrawn in 1931, the coach sections being converted into three two-car articulated sets.

THE RISE OF THE AUTO-TRAIN

Let us pause for a moment to consider, physical drawbacks apart, the sudden demise of the railmotor after it had proved to be so tremendously successful.

In the late twentieth century consumer age, vinyl records faced competition from compact cassette tapes, which had all the benefits of traditional reel-to-reel tape recorders without the awkwardness of threading tape, but all the drawbacks too, such as hiss and tape breakage. Then along comes the CD, and once the price comes down, and you can play them in the car,

A GWR 517 class tank engine 'sandwiched' on an auto train working at Lampeter. GWT

both prior formats are history. Obsolete, yes, but never actually rendered useless.

Just as the GWR was the first to embrace the railmotor concept big time, it was also the first, around the same time, to introduce push-pull operation for 'normal' trains so that they could be driven from either end, a traditional locomotive (not one built into a coach body) capable of being remotely controlled from a cab at the far end of the train, either in another locomotive or one built into the rear of an unpowered carriage (the trailing end contains the driver's vestibule).

In 1904, auto-fitted tank engines and carriages formed auto-trains on the Brentford branch as a successful experiment to see how they fared against steam railmotors. The control system

GWR 517 class 04-2T No. 1157 at Box on the daily working to Calne, about 1907. THE LATE PAUL STRONG COLLECTION

took the form of rodding.

The system allowed the control cab to be placed up to two carriages from the engine – giving a far greater capacity than steam railmotors with or without a single trailer, but having the advantages of eliminating the need to run round.

The auto-trailers were similar in design and construction to the railmotors, but off course lacking the integral steam engine.

During and after 1905, the GWR fitted several types of locomotive with auto gear, as auto-trains became a common sight across every division of the Swindon empire.

They included the 517 class 0-4-2Ts of 1868, 455 class 2-4-0Ts, which had appeared in 1869, the 1076 class 0-6-0 saddle/pannier tanks introduced in 1870, and the 2021 class 0-6-0 saddle/pannier tanks of 1897.

At first, the GWR adapted existing coaches. Auto-trailers Nos. 1 to 28 were a Heinz 57 varieties affair, comprising several different types including clerestory coaches. There were also 'intermediate' coaches, which were fitted with control transmission equipment only, and were placed between the auto-trailer and the locomotive.

Auto-trailer No. 48 was an innovative design which had sliding doors along the full length of the body operated by a guard using a handwheel which opened and closed them all at the same time.

Nos. 71 to 98 had corridor connections to allow them to run with an intermediate vehicle, allowing the guard to collect fares from both. Within the early auto-trailer fleet there were many variations: No. 45, for example, was unique in having corridor connections at its trailing end. Often ordinary coaches were converted to auto-trailers with a cab incorporated at one end. Virtually all the GWR steam railmotor carriage bodies ended up eventually being converted into auto-trailers.

Within 12 months of the Brentford branch trials, other companies such as the Midland, North Eastern and Great Central railways had experimented with different methods of push-pull operation.

If more than one autocoach was used in a train, the locomotive would often be 'sandwiched' between the coaches, to reduce play in the control linkages. Otherwise, the two coaches could 'lead' the locomotive which would push the train from the back.

A note on livery, here, in view of the both admiring and inquisitive glances received by No. 93 on its 2011 comeback. Before 1 September 1908, the GWR painted both railmotors and autocars in chocolate and cream. From that date, all coaching stock became brown, lined with gold leaf and black, and having white roofs and black underframes. From 1912-22, the brown was replaced by crimson lake, after which chocolate and cream returned. While normal coaching stock had black ends, those of both railmotors and auto-trailers carried the same colour as the side panels.

Above: *A typical Western Region auto train at Dulverton on 15 November 1962. The auto-trailer on the right,* Thrush, *was one of only two which were named.* GREAT WESTERN TRUST

Left: *Auto-trailer W231 leads the way for Collett auto tank No. 4866 past Radstock signalbox on Didcot's demonstration line.* FRANK DUMBLETON

Below: *An auto-train including auto-trailer No. 167 prepares to leave Llangollen engine first on today's Llangollen Railway.* ROBIN JONES

The most familiar type of GWR autocoach is the one introduced by Chief Mechanical Engineer Charles Collett in 1928. Indeed, it was the only purpose-built type of auto-trailer built by the GWR, as opposed to converting wooden-bodied coaches both from within its own fleet and those of companies acquired at the Grouping of 1923.

One big step forward with this design was the move away from all-wooden construction was to a wooden framework and flush fitted steel outer panels. The first 12 of the new auto-trailers was built as Lot 394 to Diagram A27: a classic example, No.163, survives on the Llangollen Railway.

'Modern' features introduced included electric lighting, sandboxes, the trademark warning gong at the driver's end, chain and bell communication and steam heating, along with the usual turn-under steps. In many ways, the design took the best from the auto-trailers of all of the companies that they inherited and evolved them into a new and hugely-successful design which lasted nearly four decades in service. The last of 163 coaches built broadly to the basic design was outshopped under British Railways in 1954.

On rural branches, at first these were paired with a 517 class locomotive, or after 1932, Collett's improvement on Locomotive Superintendent' Joseph Armstrong's design, the 4800/1400 class 0-4-2T.

A total of 75 were built over four years and were fitted with auto gear so that the fireman could remain on the footplate while the driver controlled the train from the auto-trailer cab. It is the Collett auto-tank that is most familiarly associated with the 1928 auto-trailers, and wove the romance of idyllic rural retreats that were served by them.

In the final stage of steam auto-train development, several pannier tanks were also fitted for auto working, as were several 4575 Class 2-6-2Ts from 1953 onwards.

Auto-trains became the mainstay of services on many GWR branches, particularly in rural areas. They were also used on London inner-suburban services out of Paddington, hauled by the faster and more powerful 54XX 0-6-0 panniers, while on the steep South Wales valleys lines, the smaller-wheeled 64XX types were engaged.

Auto-trains also ran on main lines, such as the route between Gloucester and Chalford, over which the first GWR steam railmotor services had famously run. Here, the auto-trailer, with its engine facing its home station of Chalford, the fireman on the footplate and the driver in the coach vestibule, would be propelled down the valley to Stonehouse. The service was extended to Gloucester in 1920, and like so many of its counterparts elsewhere on the GWR network, became part of the community. The drivers knew many passengers by name and often would wait if one of their regulars was late. Mothers called it the 'pram train' and packed the luggage compartment with pushchairs and carrycots.

They may have been small beer, but the auto-trains did not necessarily have to be slow. It was said that on the stretch of line where the Gloucester-Chalford auto-trains ran alongside

GWR prairie tanks became auto fitted under British Railways. In what could be a typical rural branch line at many places on the Western Region, No. 5526 heads a single car working towards Carrog on the Llangollen Railway on April 19 2009. ROBIN JONES

In 2011, the Bodmin & Wenford Railway reintroduced auto-trains. GWR 0-6-0PT No. 6435 is seen approaching Quarry Curve with auto-trailer No. 232. BEN HARDING/BWR

the main line as far as Standish Junction, speeds of more than 60 mph were often recorded as they raced main line expresses.

Like the railmotor and petrol-electric autocar, the auto-trailers, of which 256 had appeared on Swindon territory, marked a huge advance towards the modern railway of today, for they were the forerunner of the driving trailers used in diesel multiple units.

Incidentally, the first locomotive bought by the Great Western Society was a Collett auto-tank, No 1466.

And although British Rail's steam ban took effect from 11 August 1968, the date when the last official steam train over the national network, the '615 Guinea Special' was run, a prior booking for No. 1466 to operate on the Cholsey to Wallingford branch on 21 September that year was honoured.

Its train was auto-coach No 231, making it a type that therefore lasted until – and indeed beyond – the end of steam.

CHAPTER FIVE
THE RISE AND RISE OF THE DIESEL RAILCAR

THE SELF-PROPELLED self-contained rail vehicle had mushroomed overnight, but despite the early success of the steam railmotors and the untapped promise offered by the petrol-electric railcars, by the 1930s, for many the golden age of steam, it appeared by and large to be shunted into a siding of history.

What was needed was a type of reliable, efficient propulsion that would overcome the objections to using a steam bogie and the perceived disadvantages of the petrol engine.

The answer for those lines not able or willing to switch to electric traction lay in the great invention of German thermal engineer Rudolf Diesel, who in 1892 patented the pressure-ignited heat engine that bears his name. Four years later he demonstrated an engine with a theoretical efficiency of 75%, compared to the 10% efficiency of the steam engine, and by 1898 had become a millionaire.

At first diesel engines powered ships, submarines and pumps, but later replaced steam-powered engines in a multitude of applications, including the railway.

In 1913, manufacturers ASEA and Atlas produced a 75hp diesel railcar in Sweden, and followed up with a series of large models up to 300hp between then and 1925.

Five Sulzer-engined diesel-electric cars were delivered to Prussia and Saxony in 1914.

Diesel railcars were built in the 1920s in Czechoslovakia, Denmark and Germany, leaving Britain lagging behind, until 1928, when the London Midland & Scottish Railway built a 500hp four-car diesel-electric set. A Beardmore eight-cylinder engine similar to types used in airships powered by electrics manufacturered by Dick Kerr and built into an experimental Lancashire & Yorkshire Railway early electric unit produced Britain's first diesel-electric multiple unit. Unsuccessful in itself, it woke up British manufacturers, notably English Electric, to the need to copy the continental trends and look to the future.

In 1932, the LMS trialled Huddersfield manufacturer Karrier's Ro-Railer, a hybrid 26-seater single-decker bus capable of running on both road and rail. It took five minutes to adapt the wheels from rail to road and vice versa.

Above left: Tyneside Venturer *was the LNER's first Armstrong-Whitworth diesel railcar.* STEPHEN MIDDLETON COLLECTION

Above centre: *Armstrong-Whitworth railcar* Northumbrian *was bought by the LNER in 1934 after running trials on the LMS as well. It is seen with a trailer.* STEPHEN MIDDLETON COLLECTION

Above right: *A fourth Armstrong-Whitworth diesel-electric vehicle, 57-seater lightweight rail bus No. 294, entered service with the LNER in the Newcastle area in 1933. It is believed to have only been kept as a standby for one of the larger railcars. Its streamlined body was constructed by Park Royal.* STEPHEN MIDDLETON COLLECTION

The vehicle was tested between Hemel Hempstead and Harpenden to Redbourn, and also on the Stratford-upon-Avon & Midland Junction Railway. The LMS approached Karrier after buying a mansion on the outskirts of Stratford and converting it into the Welcombe Hotel.

The Ro-Railer collected passengers at the hotel, took them to the station and ran on the tracks from Stratford to Blisworth, Northamptonshire, linking to a London service

However, the Ro-Railer lasted only two months in service before the LMS returned the vehicle to the manufacturer, claiming that passenger loadings had been disappointing.

Meanwhile in 1931, manufacturer Armstrong Whitworth built three 60-seater Sulzer-engined diesel railcars, intended for the LMS, LNER and the Southern Railway, and named *Northumbrian*, *Tyneside Venturer* and *Lady Hamilton*.

LNER Chief Mechanical Engineer Sir Nigel Gresley watched a demonstration of *Tyneside Venturer* on 23 November 1931, and the following year it was bought and used on services around Scarborough. All three ended up in LNER service and withdrawn in 1939, were scrapped in 1944.

Next, the LMS looked to France and a rubber-tyred ten-wheeled railcar built by Michelin, which operated between Oxford and Bletchley in 1932, where it was claimed it cut 12 minutes of the normal steam-hauled timing. Amongst the reasons given by the LMS for not ordering a production batch was that it was too silent for railway lineside workers to hear approaching, and it could not haul an extra trailer or horseboxes which were then a mainstay of branch line traffic.

From obscurity to international stardom, the concept of the self-propelled railcar reached dizzy heights when in Germany in 1932, the two-car 410hp 'Flying Hamburger' set equipped with a new 12-cylinder Maybach engine reached 77mph.

Its success made steam engineers everywhere sit up and think: some of the greatest LNER and LMS Pacifics were produced partially as a reaction to its success. Seventeen more 'Flying Hamburger' sets followed in 1935/6, while by 1932, the USA had stolen a march on the UK and was operating around 700 railcars, mostly petrol-electric types.

English Electric responded in 1934 by building an experimental 200hp diesel railcar called *Bluebird* which underwent trials on the LMS between Rugby and Market Harborough and Bedford and Bletchley, but the engine suffered from big-end bearing failures.

THE GWR FLEET

Just as the Great Western Railway had gone head over heels for the steam railmotor while at the same time pioneering the successful auto-train alternative, it was the first British railway company to produce a fleet of diesel railcars. And what a fleet it was.

The GWR railcars were a milestone in UK railway history. Drawing upon the concept of the self-propelled all-in-one vehicle as epitomised by the steam railmotor, they took ideas manifested in the LNER petrol-electric autocar and early diesel railcars to dizzy new heights.

While the steam railmotors were introduced by the GWR to see off a road tram scheme, the company's diesel railcars drew heavily on developments in road transport, which by the early thirties was rapidly emerging as a serious threat to branch line and freight traffic.

The GWR railcars were invented by Mr C. F. Cleaver of Hardy Motors Ltd., a subsidiary of the Associated Equipment Company Ltd.

AEC had already built petrol and diesel-engined shunting locomotives along with lorries and tractors through associated firm the Four Wheel Drive Lorry Company. Cleaver looked at AEC's 130 bhp six-cylinder diesel engine used in London buses of the day along with other

GWR diesel railcar W4W, now a static exhibit in Swindon's STEAM museum. ROBIN JONES

Note the difference between the angular design of GWR diesel railcar No. 22, seen on the traverser at Didcot, and the earlier air-smoothed outlines of W4W. FRANK DUMBELTON

commercial vehicles, and drew up plans for a lightweight self-propelled vehicle. He also saw that streamlining, an innovation not available to the steam railmotors, would improve the railcars' performance. A prototype car, No. 1, was based loosely on the German 'Flying Hambuger' diesel unit, but with a more refined air-smoothed appearance designed after windtunnel tests were carried out at the London Passenger Transport Board's Chiswick laboratory. The rounded lines and yellow and brown livery of these first GWR railcars built led to their nickname of "Flying Bananas".

The 69-seater 62ft 9in long railcar was fitted with an 8.85 litre diesel engine, which powered a five-speed pre-selective gearbox with a fluid flywheel to drive to a pair of axleboxes on one side of the railcar. It had a maximum speed of 63mph and as with the railmotors and auto-trains,could be controlled from either end.

The bodywork was provided by Park Royal Coachworks of Willesden, another AEC subsidiary. Maximum speed was 63 mph with control shared between the ends of the railcar. The GWR was sufficiently impressed by the railcar to display No. 1 at the International Commercial Motor Transport Exhibition at Olympia in November 1933. It was a huge hit amongst visitors.

The first official run was from Paddington to Reading on 1 December 1933. Ever conscious of the value of publicity, a large contingent of newspaper reporters were on board. AEC described the first run as an "unqualified triumph."

No. 1 entered public service three days later, running from Slough shed to Windsor and Didcot. Before the end of the year, however, it was taken out of service for minor adjustments, including refinements to the braking system and engine mounting.

The opportunity was taken to fit automatic train control.

It was back in traffic in February 1934, and in its first year in service, the 24-ton vehicle carried 136,000 passengers and clocked up around 60,000 miles.

As with the Golden Valley steam railmotors three decades before, the GWR realised that it was on to a winner, and in February 1934 asked AEC to build six more diesel railcars. For this batch, two AEC 8.85-litre engines were installed, giving the railcars a maximum speed of 80mph.

Railcars Nos. 2-4 were equipped with a buffet bar to fit in with their intended use on an express businessman's service between Birmingham and Cardiff. Each contained a lavatory with hot water heated by the engines' exhausts. Cleaver oversaw their construction at AEC while Park Royal produced the bodywork. A press trip from Paddington to Oxford on 3 July saw the 44 miles covered in 40 minutes, and the next day, on a run from Paddington to Birmingham Snow Hill, 76mph was reached near Princes Risborough.

These three 44-seater railcars entered service on 16 July. They provided the first regular fast scheduled diesel service in Britain and took two hours 22 minutes to cover the 116½ miles from Birmingham to Cardiff with stops at Gloucester and Newport, and an average speed of 49.3mph. Despite their sleekness and modernity, third class fares were charged.

In 1935, three more railcars were built, 70 seaters for suburban traffic, with bodywork made by the Gloucester Carriage & Wagon Company. Another ten were supplied the following year, the last of which, No. 17, was a parcels car for use between Southall and

Below left: *A GWR diesel railcar in the early British Railways carmine and cream livery pauses at Dymock, Gloucestershire. In Edwardian times, such services would have been handled by steam railmotors.* GREAT WESTERN TRUST

Below right: *GWR railcar No. 16 in service.* GWS

Oxford. Offloading parcels on to a purpose-built self-contained unit was seen as a way of cutting loading times at stations for ordinary passenger trains.

By 1936, the railcars accounted for three per cent of the daily passenger mileage of the entire GWR system, with all 17 cars running a combined mileage of more than a million miles.

The Weymouth railcar service recorded a speed of 65.8mph between Castle Cary and Westbury. Clearly, here was a serious commercial threat to steam haulage.

In 1937, a new type of diesel railcar was produced. No. 18 had a stronger chassis than its predecessors, was reduced to 49 seats and was fitted with standard buffers and drawgear, capable of hauling at least two coaches or eight horseboxes. During trials in April between Brentford and Southall, it hauled four trailer cars. It was intended for use on the branch between Lambourn and Newbury, and had to be able to haul horseboxes as well as provide a passenger service.

Electro-pneumatic controls were fitted so that they could be controlled from trailer cars that had been fitted with a driver's cab, and importantly in terms of historical development, for multiple unit operation.

The next 20 railcars, which completed the GWR fleet, were built by Swindon Works, to a different and angular body design, which was more functional than the streamlined

The evolution continues: GWR railcar No. 22 alongside British Railways Class 121 'bubblecar' No.55034 at Didcot. FRANK DUMBLETON

predecessors. Nos. 19-33 were intended for use on previously loss-making branch lines, where the steam railmotors had in their day worked miracles, but could still be used on the main line routes when required. The first of these 48-seater railcars was introduced in June 1940. No. 34 was built to a similar design. It was virtually the same as Nos. 19-33 except it was used for express parcels. Unlike No. 17, it could also pull vans.

The last four, Nos. 35-38, were designed to work in pairs with a trailer car in between, and so had only one driving compartment in the front and rear vehicle. They could carry 104 passengers, or 184 with a carriage in the middle. They entered service from November 1941.

In 1944, railcars Nos. 6 and 19 were loaned to the LNER.

The first GWR railcar to be withdrawn was No. 9, after it caught fire at Heyford in July 1945.

As with the steam railmotors, the GWR diesel railcars were a victim of their own success. By 1945, the buffet cars on the Birmingham route could not cope with demand and were relegated to the less patronised Reading to Bristol route.

At nationalisation, the railcars were repainted from GWR chocolate and cream to crimson lake and cream. The last 13 in service were withdrawn in 1962. Three are preserved: W4W at STEAM – Museum of the Great Western Railway in Swindon, No. 20 on the Kent & East Sussex Railway and No. 22 at Didcot Railway Centre.

Railcars had by then long been in service in the USA and on the continent. However, it was the GWR that had firmly established their permanent use in Britain, in so many ways the successor to the steam railmotor.

One of the last GWR railcars in British Railway service is seen at Burlish Halt between Bewdley and Stourport-on-Severn. GREAT WESTERN TRUST

THE AGE OF THE DMU

Watching the huge success of the GWR railcars, in 1938 the LMS built a three-car aluminium streamlined articulated diesel railcar set at Derby, each car being powered by two Leyland 125hp engines. Numbered 80000/80001/80002, it was first used between Oxford and Cambridge, but did not increase revenue, and was switched to the St Pancras-Bedford-Nottingham route.

It may in itself have been the next stage of development of DMU sets in the UK, but after World War Two broke out, it had little chance as a 'one off'. Withdrawn in 1940, it was converted to an electrification maintenance unit in 1949, and was last heard of in a derelict state in 1967.

The LMS DMU set of 1938 may well have paved the way for future designs if it had not been for World War Two. NRM

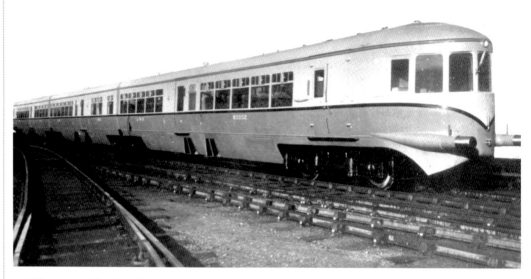

The LMS DMU set of 1938 may well have paved the way for future designs if it had not been for World War Two. NRM

When the 'Big Four' companies were nationalised on 1 January 1948, there were a total of just 37 diesel railcars in the British Railways fleet; 35 GWR vehicles and two Armstrong Whitworth cars built for the LNER.

Their distinct advantages were by now clear, but in war-ravaged Britain, the first priority was to make good the losses suffered by the rail network during years of minimal maintenance and enemy action. Also, the emphasis was still almost exclusively on steam, because of a global oil shortage.

The self-contained self-powered vehicle was, however now here to stay. The replacement of the steam unit by an efficient diesel alternative had eradicated most of the disadvantages of the railmotor and would clearly supersede the auto train sooner or later.

As the years of postwar austerity waned, the chance would arise for the replacement of steam trains by 'modern' traction. The opportunity presented itself with the appointment of a committee, under a Railway Executive memorandum of 9 August 1951, to consider the scope for the use of lightweight trains. It was headed by H.G. Bowles of the Western Region, the successor to the GWR, and looked at the use of diesel railcars in Europe, where by then more than 3,000 such vehicles were in service.

In 1952, the committee produced a report which recommended the building and trial of lightweight DMUs, which, it said, could cut the cost of the equivalent steam services by more than half.

Three areas were chosen as testbeds – Leeds, Lincolnshire and West Cumberland. It was also recommended that diesel railcars be used to replace auto trains on 168 routes.

In November 1952, Derby's carriage and wagon works was asked to build eight two-car sets for the West Riding and 13 more for West Cumberland. The first 16 power cars with fitted with two Leyland six-cylinder horizontal type 125hp engines, and had a maximum speed of 62mph.

The first of the DMU sets was demonstrated with a trial run from Marylebone to Beaconsfield and return on April 29 1954. In Yorkshire, the first service was launched on 14 June 1954 between Leeds and Bradford and was an instant success. However, in hilly West Cumberland, the initial 13 two-car sets, fitted with AEC 150hp diesel engines, suffered at first because of wintry weather and the lack of anti-freeze.

In 1952, the private sector entered the world of DMU building when the British United Traction Company built four-wheeled lightweight cars powered by AEC 125hp engines. Demonstrated at Gerrards Cross, they entered service around Wellingborough and ended up running services on the Watford-St Albans route until withdrawal in 1963.

Meanwhile, the postwar economy continued to improve, and taking on board the results

This rare picture shows a three-car set formed from a series of four-wheeled railcars built by the British United Traction Company in 1952. There were 11 vehicles in all, seven powered cars, each driven by one AEC 125hp diesel engine with a fluid flywheel, and four trailers. They were built just as fuel rationing was ending after the war and thoughts were turning towards the development of diesel units. This was the first set to be built which was delivered in grey livery and it may have been its first running trial. The schoolboy trainspotters are captivated by it as it would have been unlike anything they had seen before.
ROBIN JONES COLLECTION

This three-car Class 101 DMU was built by Metropolitan Cammell in 1956 as part of one of its many orders under the Modernisation Plan and it was still operating on network routes around Manchester in 2003. FRED KERR

The 1955 Modernisation Plan initiated a program of building 4,600 multiple unit trainsets in one, two, three or four-car combinations from a variety of builders which could be further combined as necessary to provide longer trainsets. This six-car trainset running on the Severn Valley Railway in October 2004 has two Class 118 vehicles built by Birmingham Railway Carriage & Wagon Works and three Class 108 vehicles and a Class 114 vehicle built by Derby Carriage & Wagon Works, all operated from one driving panel in the leading vehicle. FRED KERR

from these early trials, on 1 December 1954, British Railways unveiled its blueprint for the future. It produced a report entitled Modernisation and Re-Equipment of the British Railways, or the 1955 Modernisation Plan for short, and faced with ever-stiffening competition from road transport, aimed to boost speed, reliability, safety and line capacity, while making services more attractive to passengers and freight operators.

The most distinctive feature of the report was the complete phasing out of steam locomotives by diesel and electric alternatives. It also proposed the electrification of principal main lines, including the East Coast Main Line to Leeds and possibly York, the Great Northern suburban system, Euston to Birmingham/Manchester/Liverpool, Chelmsford to Clacton/Ipswich/Felixstowe; the Liverpool Street north-east suburban system; Fenchurch Street to Tilbury and Shoeburyness; and the Glasgow north suburban network.

The Railway Executive's initial plan to keep steam on busy routes until it was superseded by electric traction was abandoned, and instead, diesels would provide a stop-gap until electrification, while on secondary lines, they would provide the long-term solution. There was a three-year plan to introduce up to 4,600 diesel railcars, built both by British Railways and the private sector, which, as with the case of the corresponding new main line diesel locomotives, led to a rich variety of different types being turned out.

The report proposed to spend £1,240-million over 15 years to achieve these goals.

In 1956, a government White Paper confidently stated that modernisation would help eliminate BR's financial deficit by 1962.

Two diesel railcar vehicle lengths were planned, 57ft for the London Midland and North Eastern regions, and 63ft 6in for the Western, Eastern and Scottish regions.

The next major batch of DMUs came from Derby Works, which produced sets for use in both the Midlands and East Anglia. In total, Derby eventually turned out 122 lightweight power cars and 95 driving trailers.

The first of the longer-bodied vehicles was built by Swindon for the Scottish Region. It supplied 21 three-car 158-seater Inter-City sets equipped with a pair of AEC 150hp engines in each power car for use between Glasgow and Edinburgh, with a first-class corridor coach or buffet car in the centre. The first set of what later became Class 156 was unveiled at Swindon on 27 July 1956.

Many initial problems with diesel railcars being introduced across the national network were down to the fact that they were being introduced to steam infrastructure, in which they sat uncomfortably. However, in 1955 Derby opened the first diesel training school and new maintenance depots were opened at Lincoln and Norwich by the Eastern Region.

In 1956, plans for a fast Inter City service between Liverpool and Leeds were announced. Derby built an experimental pair of diesel-electric railcars using underframes and bogies from former Euston-Watford EMU stock of 1926, and fitted with Paxman six-cylinder engines.

The initial programme of DMU trainsets, begun by British Railways in 1952, included two single car vehicles which could be combined to operate as a two-car trainset and were initially allocated to work Banbury-Buckingham services. Car No. 79900 was saved for preservation and restored to as-new condition for use on the Ecclesbourne Valley Railway at Wirksworth. ROBIN JONES

The initial DMU programme, begun by British Railways in 1952, also included several four-wheeled railbuses for light branch lines which were supplied by private manufacturers including the German firm of Waagen und Maschinenbau. A pair were bought by the nascent Keighley & Worth Valley Railway to operate local services. The sight of No. 79964 operating in January 2009 shows how useful these vehicles can be – if operated under the right conditions on the right lines. FRED KERR

The set's first trial run in September 1956 saw it cover the 129 miles from Derby to St Pancras in 120 minutes. Another run, from Derby to Gloucester, saw it tackle the 1-in-37 Lickey Incline at 37mph. Eventually it ended up in regular service between Derby and Carlisle, but because of its weight and build cost, no further examples were built.

In 1960, Swindon built DMUs, later known as Class 124s, for the trans-Pennine route.

It is outside the scope of this book to describe all of the different variations of DMU designed and produced at this time, but they broadly fell into five categories.

Firstly, there were the low-density units such as Class 101 DMUs which, like the steam railmotors before them, were designed for use on rural lines and provincial commuter services. They were initially allocated to all parts of the network except the Western and Southern regions.

Secondly, there were 'high-density' units like the Class 121s which were intended for the busy commuter services into London, and also for local services in Birmingham and Liverpool and throughout the Western Region. These were single-car vehicles, nicknamed 'bubblecars',

which could also pull trailers, just like some of the more advanced early steam railmotors.

Thirdly, there were cross-country units, which were basically low density units with more luxurious seating, and first allocated to the Western and Scottish Regions.

Then there were Inter City units built for express services on the important secondary routes on the Western, Scottish and North Eastern regions, which shared many features with the locomotive-hauled coaching stock of the day.

Finally, there were parcels cars. Like the GWR forerunners, they were single cars with a cab at each end, and were built for the Western and London Midland Regions.

Over and above these types were the Diesel Electric Multiple Units developed during the fifties and sixties for the Southern Region, where third-rail electrification was expanding, and diesel units were needed for the remaining non-electrified lines. Diesel-mechanical and diesel-hydraulic units were judged to have inadequate acceleration, which would have caused delays to other traffic when operating on electrified lines. The Southern DEMUs included classes 205 and 207, nicknamed 'Thumpers' because of their unique sound.

One of the very economical but short-lived AC Railbus four-wheelers at Bodmin North. GREAT WESTERN TRUST

In addition, there were single-car railbuses provided by private manufacturers. Already mentioned are the British United Traction Company's pioneer four-wheelers of 1952. Six years later, five different manufacturers turned out a total of 22 vehicles, the aim being to provide 'minimalist' units for lightly-used branch lines where even normal DMUs were said to be uneconomic. In this respect, these may be considered to be the direct descendants of the steam railmotor.

Sports car manufacturer AC Cars of Thames Ditton turned out five 46-seater four-wheel railbuses fitted with AEC 150hp engines, the first, W79979, delivered to the Western Region in February 1958. They famously worked on the Kemble to Cirencester and Tetbury branches and around Bodmin and Yeovil, and were the subject of a popular pocket-money Airfix 00 scale kit. The last was withdrawn from Scotland on 27 January 1967, not even lasting until the end of steam that August.

The AC railbuses were followed by five 56-seater railbuses built by Waggon and Machinenbau of Donauworth and originally fitted with Buessing 150hp engines. They lasted on routes in East Anglia until 1964.

In July 1958, Park Royal Vehicles delivered five 50-seater railbuses with AEC 150hp engines to the London Midland Region and, transferred to Scotland two years later, lasted until 1968. Wickham of Ware built five railcars with Meadows 150hp engines. The lightest

Preserved Southern Region Class 201 'Hastings' diesel electric multiple Unit No. 11 passes Corfe Castle en route to Swanage with a main line railtour on 25 June 2011. The 'Hastings' units, nicknamed 'Slim Jims', were built with narrow bodies because of the tight clearances on the cheaply-built Tunbridge Wells-Hastings line. ANDREW P.M. WRIGHT

A Class 124 Trans-Pennine DMU set leaves Liverpool Lime Street on 1 November 1975. Sadly, unlike its ancestor the GWR railmotor, not one example of this type has survived into preservation. BRIAN SHARPE

of the railbuses at just 11.2 tons, they seated 44 passengers and went to the Scottish Region. They too had gone by 1968.

Finally, Bristol Commercial Vehicles delivered a pair of railbuses which ran in Scotland for a decade.

Just as with the steam railmotors half a century before, DMUs were welcomed by the public and were by and large successful. By the end of 1959, with nearly 2,000 power cars in service, 'modern' traction accounted for half of all route mileage. However, they could not prevent the closure of lossmaking branch lines due increased competition from road transport.

The closures that came both before, during and after the reign of Dr Richard Beeching led to many of the new DMUs quickly becoming redundant and switched to other routes. There was also a cutback in the amount of DMUs that were built: out of the 4,600 railcars promised in the 1955 Modernisation Plan, only 4,171 were built.

For the doomed country branch lines, even a steam railmotor could not have saved the day! However, on the lines that remained – and Britain still has one of the most intensive rail networks of any country – more and more territory was being claimed by the DMU, the direct descendant of the railmotor, and its 'sister' the EMU.

THE BLUE PULLMAN

The finest and most iconic of all the British Railways first generation DMUs was without a doubt the Blue Pullman.

If we view the steam railmotor as a horse and cart, its DMU descendant the Blue Pullman must be considered a jet airliner by comparison.

The Blue Pullman came off the British Transport Commission drawing board in 1957, when it was announced that Metro Cammell would produce five sets for operation. As part of the 1955 Modernisation Plan, the British Transport Commission and the Pullman Car Company, which had become part of the nationalised railway in 1954, formed a committee to examine the possibility of running diesel express passenger services using new trains.

Branded with the classic Pullman hallmark of utmost quality, the new diesel trains were intended to offer standards of service never before seen on a British train, bettering even the luxury trains of the thirties on the LNER, LMS and GWR. They offered meals at every seat, air conditioning, and a staffing level good enough to ensure that passengers would want for nothing. Indeed, the Blue Pullman, designed for a maximum speed of 90mph, looked more towards the comforts and style associated with aircraft than traditional railway carriages.

There were two versions: two six-car sets for the London Midland Region and three eight-car sets for the Western Region. The first set appeared for trials in October 1959.

The sets were originally formed in six- or eight-car lengths and comprised three basic types of carriage: the motor car, kitchen car and parlour car. In service the cars were permanently coupled and hermetically sealed for maintenance of the air-conditioning settings.

There was a power car at each end. They were powered by two GEC 199hp traction motors, with another two on the adjoining car.

The Blue Pullmans entered Monday to Friday service on 23 July 1960 with the St Pancras to Manchester Central service on the London Midland Region, and on the Western Region, where steam railmotors had long been a distant memory, on 12 September that year. The Western Region initially operated them from Wolverhampton Low Level to Paddington and Bristol to Paddington, with a service from Paddington to Cardiff and Swansea beginning in 1961.

For British Railways, the Blue Pullman had the desired effect: the publicity that they generated sent out the message that train travel would not automatically be consigned by progress to the dustbin of history along with the steam locomotive, and that they could provide the transport of the future in which the car would nonetheless be undisputed king.

However, the new bogie design proved to be an Achilles heel. It had been successfully tested under standard Mk1 coaching stock, but the weight difference between a Mk1 and a heavy Pullman was too great, and complaints over ride quality would persist throughout the

Railmotor descendant the Blue Pullman: a Western Region set is seen passing Acocks Green in Birmingham in 1963. MICHAEL MENSING

life of the trains.

With the electrification of the West Coast Main Line to Manchester, the London Midland services ended and the sets were transferred to the Western Region.

However, just as with the railmotors, technology was bypassing the Blue Pullmans as they reached their zenith. By the late 1960s, ordinary Mk2 coaching stock was in regular use, making air-conditioned travel available to the masses, without the payment of supplementary fares, weakening the advantages that the Blue Pullman offered. There were talks about withdrawing them as early as 1969, but three sets on the Paddington to Bristol and Cardiff services soldiered on until 1973. All of them were scrapped in 1975, and sadly not a single car was preserved.

THE ADVANCED PASSENGER TRAIN

While the iconic Blue Pullman did not pass the test of time, it undoubtedly helped establish the express passenger DMU concept as the preferred way forward for British Rail, which in the sixties had been looking at other high-speed trains around the world, like Japan's Shinkansen 'bullet train' and France's TGV, to see what could be developed as a British version.

The answer was the prototype Advanced Passenger Train tilting train unit, or Advanced Passenger Train Experimental (APT-E). Just as the steam bogie of the railmotors had given way to the diesel engine of the GWR railcars, so in the case of the APT-E, gas turbines, a lighter form of traction, replaced diesel.

In order to allow a top speed of 155 mph, British Rail's Derby Research Division drew on aero engineering principles and developed an advanced active tilting technology, using hydraulic rams controlled by spirit level sensors to tilt the passenger cars into the curves so that no lateral forces would be felt.

The APT-E was the only British Rail multiple unit to be powered by gas turbines. It consisted of two driving power cars (PC1/2), each fitted with four Leyland 350 gas turbines and two trailer cars (TC1/2).

Its first run came on 25 July 1972, from Derby to Duffield, and immediately ran into union opposition over the operation of trains by a single man – a jump that even the steam

A working party at Shildon's Locomotion museum helps maintain British Rail's only gas turbine multiple unit, the APT-E. ANTHONY COULLS

railmotors had not made. That delayed its second run until August 1973.

Between Swindon and Reading on 10 August 1975, APT-E reached 152.3 mph. However, it never entered public service or production and in June 1976 was handed to the National Railway Museum at York for preservation.

As an experiment it was deemed a success. However, Leyland had ceased production of gas turbines and with no alternative available, the ensuing APT-P and APT-S trains were electrically powered by overhead pick-up.

The three production APT-P trains were launched in 1981, the first public run taking place on 7 December from Glasgow Central to Euston. However, it was felt that they were rushed into service before they were ready because of political pressures. The return trip saw some cars suffer tilt failures, and the cold weather of the harsh winter of 1981/2 saw brakes freeze. The APT-Ps were taken out of service four days later.

The APT-Ps re-entered service in the middle of 1984 and ran regularly, but time was moving on, and there was disinterest in the project from the higher echelons of British Rail. Two of the units were quietly withdrawn and scrapped, while one ended up on static display at Crewe Heritage Centre where it stands today.

It was not all in vain. Tilting technology developed for the APT found its way into the Virgin Trains Class 390 Pendolino EMUs built in the twenty-first century for the West Coast Main Line.

THE BEST OF THEM ALL?

While the development of the Advanced Passenger Train was proceeding, British Rail top brass looked around for a 'stop-gap' type of inter-city express train, that would bridge the gap between the first generation DMUs and the proposed APTs.

The end result was arguably the most successful class of passenger traction in the history of Britain's railways – the InterCity Class 125 High Speed Train.

In 1970 it was decided to build two lightweight Bo-Bo locomotives to top and tail a rake of the new Mk3 coaches. As such, it is debatable as to whether it is a true DMU in the perfect sense of the term, but the locomotives could not be used to haul other trains, and retained the double-ended design that was a basic principle of the steam railmotor.

Drawing on many of the lessons learned from the Blue Pullman but not necessarily including its design features, the prototype train of seven coaches and two

locomotives was completed in August 1972 and within weeks was running trials on the main line. In May 1973, the prototype set a world diesel speed record of 143.2 mph.

Three more years of trials led to British Rail's decision to build 27 production High Speed Trains for InterCity services between Paddington, Bristol, and South Wales. The first production power car, No. 43002, was delivered in late 1975, and in October 1976, a 125mph service began on the Western Region. By May 1977, all 27 units were working and had completely replaced locomotive-hauled trains on the Bristol and South Wales routes.

Until the coming of the High Speed Train, the maximum speed of British trains was limited to 100 mph. The HST allowed a 25% increase in service speeds along many lines they operated. Again, as with the railmotor, the innovation was a huge success, with passengers responding very favourably, helped in this case by British Rail's TV adverts 'This is the age of the train' with disc jockey Jimmy Saville.

The displacement by High Speed Trains of the late sixties Class 50 diesel-electric locomotives to slower services effectively finished off the last Western Region Class 52 Western diesel-hydraulic locomotives by early 1977.

The HSTs then began replacing the glamorous Class 55 Deltic locomotives on the East Coast Main Line, taking over no less than the 'Flying Scotsman' service from King's Cross to Edinburgh from May 1978.

By 1982, when production ended, 95 High Speed Train sets including 197 Class 43 power cars had been built.

A world speed record for a diesel train carrying passengers was set on 27 September 1985, when a seven-car set forming a special press train for the launch of a new Tees-Tyne Pullman service from Newcastle to King's Cross hit 144mph north of York. The record for the world's fastest diesel-powered train was set by a Class 125 unit on 1 November 1987 when it reached 148mph while descending Stoke Bank on the East Coast Main Line in Lincolnshire with a test run for a new type of bogie later to be used under Mk4 coaches.

The Class 125s brought sizeable improvements in services, and at the time of writing, many of the post-privatisation Train Operating Companies still have them in service. Thirty five years on, they are still looking very good indeed, with performances to match.

William Bridges Adams would certainly have smiled.

Chiltern Railways has found that heavily-refurbished 1960-design first-generation single unit railcars are the ideal vehicles for working off-peak services on the Aylesbury to Princes Risborough branch line today. Unit W55034 approaches Little Kimble on 3 June 2011. ADRIAN KNOWLES

THE NEXT GENERATION

Progress is such that just as steam railmotors and auto-trains have passed into history, so it would be the turn of the first generation British Railways DMUs. It was widely accepted that while at first they were welcomed by the public, by the early eighties they had reached their sell-by date, with soaring maintenance costs, poor reliability and a dissatisfied commuter market.

First Great Western Class 150 No. 150221 is seen doing the same job as might once have been delegated to a steam railmotor, leaving St Ives with the 1.25pm to St Erth. FGW

A pair of First Great Western Class 142 Pacer units at Exeter St David's depot. ROBIN JONES

Above left: *Arriva Cross Country Trains Class 170 DMU No. 170 523 enters Leicester station.* ROBIN JONES

Above right: *Looking every bit like the Class 91 locomotive powering the train, Driver Vehicle Trailer No. 82201 is seen at the 'rear' end of an East Coast service departing Peterborough.* ROBIN JONES

At first, British Rail turned some services back over to locomotive haulage, but this pushed up operating costs. So in the mid-eighties, British Rail set out on it 'Sprinterisation' programme, to introduce three new types of DMU.

Firstly, there were the Classes 140-144 Pacer railbuses, budget-priced diesel-mechanical units utilising a four-wheeled chassis and lightweight bus bodywork, designed for branch line and stopping services. There were certainly railmotor era echoes here!

Then there were the diesel-hydraulic Sprinters: the Class 150s for branch line and commuter services, the Class 153/155/156 Super Sprinters for longer cross country services and Class 158/159 Express units for secondary express services.

Finally, there were the Networker diesel-hydraulic units, comprising the Class 165 Network Turbo for basic commuter routes, and the Class 166 Network Express for longer distance commuter services, all of which replaced first generation DMUs on the remaining non-electric commuter services into London.

Privatisation of the rail network in the nineties preceded the development of several other DMU classes. The most common were the Class 168 Clubman and Class 170/171 Turbostar units, an evolution of the Networkers and built by Bombardier Transportation, the first appearing two years after privatisation.

The Class 175 Coradia was builder Alstom's answer to the Class 170 Turbostar, but found favour only with First North Western, while First Great Western were exclusive buyers of the same manufacturer's Class 180 Adelante. First TransPennine Express services used the Siemens-designed Class 185 Desiro.

Today, most all non-electric inter-city services are currently operated by diesel electric multiple units, the venerable Class 125s now rubbing shoulders with high-speed Bombardier express units including the non-tilting Class 220 Voyager, the tilting Class 221

Super-Voyager and Class 222 Meridian/Pioneers.

Try as they might with their sleek outlines, candystripe liveries, air conditioning and sliding doors, they all hark back to an Edwardian manifestation of a mid-Victorian concept, of which the Great Western Society's steam railmotor No. 93 is now the shining and sole UK example.

While EMU development largely paralleled that of the steam railmotor/auto-train/diesel railcar/DMU dynasty, it also took many of its ideas on board.

The modern-day successor to the auto-coach, developed to overcome railmotor limitations, is the Driving Van Trailer seen on InterCity 225 express passenger trains at the opposite end from the Class 91 locomotives, which they closely resemble.

The search for replacement DMU vehicles in the early 1980s saw the testing of Leyland National bus bodies located on a rail-borne chassis as a cheap method of construction — very much echoing some of the rationale behind the steam railmotors. One of the early prototypes was LEV1 (Leyland Evaluation Vehicle No 1) seen in August 2004 on the North Norfolk Railway, where it has now been preserved. FRED KERR

The most recent example of lightweight railcars includes the flywheel-driven Parry People Mover, a pair of which have been operating the shuttle service between Stourbridge Junction and Stourbridge Town. FRED KERR

CHAPTER SIX
REBUILDING A RAILMOTOR

AS THE END OF STEAM operations on British Railways approached, eyebrows were not only being raised at the failure of the National Collection, the Science Museum's list of rolling stock to be officially preserved, to save much-loved big-name locomotives. Four schoolboys trainspotting at Southall in 1961, Angus Davis, Graham Perry, Mike Peart and Jon Barlow, were angry that not one example of a GWR Collett 14XX auto tank had been listed – and so decided to save one by themselves.

A letter published in *The Railway Magazine* led to an influx of donations from like-minded enthusiasts. The move not only led to the saving of No. 1466 but the formation of the Great Western Society in the same year.

A surge of interest led to branches of the society being formed at locations around the Swindon empire, where other locomotives and rolling stock subsequently saved by the group were stored: they included Bodmin General, the Totnes Quay branch and Taunton.

With more and more locomotives being withdrawn and sent for scrap, the society stepped up fundraising efforts to save as many as possible, but needed a bigger central site. Eventually British Rail offered the society the use of the engine shed at Didcot that had become redundant.

The society moved in with three locomotives and several carriages in 1967, laying the foundations for Didcot Railway Centre, which today houses nearly 30 locomotives.

Steam died on British Rail, but nobody seems to have told the society to apply the brakes in its efforts. Over the years, it has produced many engineering miracles: the completion of an inherited project to build a new Daniel Gooch broad gauge Firefly class 2-2-2 *Fire Fly*, together with its own demonstration line, the repatriation of GWR 4-6-0 No. 4079 *Pendennis Castle* from Australia, to which it had been exported in 1976, and, in March 2011, the completion of the restoration of a single-chimneyed King 4-6-0, No. 6023 *King Edward II*, in early British Railways experimental express passenger blue livery, from what was effectively a pile of scrap with the driving wheels cut through.

Visitors to Didcot Railway Centre for the launch into traffic of GWR 4-6-0 No. 6023 King Edward II *on 2 April 2011 after the Great Western Society rebuilt it from little more than a heap of scrap marvel at the fact it had been achieved despite its driving wheels having been cut.* ROBIN JONES

FILLING IN THE MISSING GAPS

Not content with saving examples of GWR engineering tradition, the society has continued it in its own right. Rather than merely saving old GWR locomotives, it has been actively engaged on building new ones.

Drawing on the GWR policy from the Churchward era onwards of standard components which fitted several different types of locomotive classes, schemes were drawn up to recreate extinct GWR types using remaining rusting hulks from Dai Woodham's legendary scrapyard at Barry.

In this respect, the society has become an established world leader. Scheduled for completion in 2012 is a project to 'back convert' GWR 4-6-0 No. 5942 *Maindy Hall* into the predecessor of the Hall class, a Saint, in the form of No. 2999 *Lady of Legend*.

Also ongoing is a project to replicate Hawksworth County 4-6-0 No. 1014 *County of Glamorgan* using parts from the 'Barry Ten', a pool of some of the last locomotives in Woodham Brothers' scrapyard bought with public grant aid for an abortive Welsh national railway museum project in Cardiff. An associated project at the Llangollen Railway is the building of a new Grange 4-6-0, No. 6880 *Betton Grange*, by a separate group also using 'Barry Ten' parts, while the Great Western Society is also beginning a 47XX 2-8-0 scheme on similar lines. More about these projects can be found in the companion volume *Steam's New Dawn* also published by Halsgrove.

Yet one idea in the minds of society officials preceded all of these. It dated back to 1970, when a dilapidated old coach body was acquired from British Rail.

It was no less than the sole surviving body of a GWR railmotor, No. 93 to be precise.

Withdrawn in 1934, the power bogie had been removed and scrapped. Yet the coach body survived by being converted into auto-trailer No. 212 that year.

THE RAILMOTOR WITH MANY LIVES

Built in 1908 to Diagram R, Lot 1142, as part of the last batch of GWR steam railmotors, and beginning its life working in the West London area from Southall shed, where it was likely to have been used to ferry spectators to the 1908 Olympics at the White City Stadium, No. 93 had several spells working in the West Midlands from Stourbridge shed and around the Bristol area.

During its working life it also spent time stationed at Pontypool Road, Whitland, Croes Newydd, Gloucester, Reading and Taunton. There were also a number of lengthy periods stopped, the longest of which was 374 days in 1916/17 but this may have been more to do with World War One than any mechanical problem.

Details of the coach body's later career as an auto-coach remain sketchy. A miraculous survivor, when the auto-coach was taken out of service in May 1956, it was not broken up, but converted into a departmental work-study coach for the Chief Mechanical & Electrical Engineers Department at Swindon and renumbered 079014.

Society member Ken Gibbs recalled working from that office, when it was first based at the Carriage & Wagon Department at Swindon for about 18 months.

Right: The story begins anew: auto-coach No. 212 formerly railmotor No. 93 is delivered to Didcot in 1970. GWS

Far right: The trailer for the railmotor was acquired by the Great Western Society several years before auto-coach No. 212. It is seen in early stages of preservation at Taunton in 1976. GWS

The coach's next move was to Reading where it was used by the 'Outdoor Machinery' Section. Next stop was the works at Wolverhampton, after the vehicle had been checked over at Worcester Carriage & Wagon Section to certify suitability for main line running to get there.

The works closed in 1962 and the coach moved to Lawley Street goods depot in Birmingham. The works area came under the control of the London Midland Region and the vehicle was again moved, spending time at Ashford in Kent.

There, it was examined by an LMR inspector on behalf of one of the embryonic preserved railways but he completely condemned it, the heritage line immediately losing interest.

However, the coach was moved on several other occasions before being finally withdrawn from Old Oak Common in 1970 and purchased by the society.

The society was fully aware of its history from the outset, and members said that one day it should be restored as a railmotor in its own right. However, back in 1970, the preservation movement was still very much in its infancy by today's standards, and such ambitions were no more than wishful thinking.

Not only was there no steam bogie available, but all the seats and interior fittings had been removed in 1956, so it was always going to be a project that would be 'put off until tomorrow'.

During the seventies and eighties, the coach gained another lease of life – as staff accommodation as Didcot Railway Centre began taking shape. It was stored outdoors in a siding near to Didcot Halt on one of the centre's running lines, and taking low priority, its condition inevitably deteriorated.

At one stage, the final end for the coach appeared nigh. It was set on fire as a result of a frying pan being left on a burner one evening.

Staff spotted the blaze in the nick of time and with the help of the fire brigade saved the coach, but the end result was that it looked in a worse state than ever before.

Eventually, interest in the coach within the society ranks mushroomed to the point where on 8 June 1993, a meeting at Didcot, chaired by deputy chairman Richard Croucher, saw the Steam Railmotor Project born.

Trailer No. 92 photographed in its final days of passenger service carrying early BR carmine and cream livery. The corridor connection is an original feature enabling the trailer to be coupled to an intermediate coach fitted with auto gear so that a single conductor could attend to the whole train. GWS

BLUEPRINT FOR REVIVAL

As soon as the coach body was bought, it was realised that the biggest obstacle would be the need to build a new engine unit or power bogie to replace the one scrapped in the 1930s. By the 1990s, the preservation movement had matured to the point where a number of new-build projects had been completed, notably two new double Fairlies on the Ffestiniog Railway in *Earl of Merioneth* and *David Lloyd George*, the Museum of Science & Industry's replica of Liverpool & Manchester Railway 2-2-0 *Planet*, Locomotion Enterprises' working replica of

Stephenson's *Rocket* at the National Railway Museum which also had a replica of GWR broad gauge 4-2-2 *Iron Duke*. Thanks to these, the railmotor pipedream was now practical, in theory at least.

From the start of the project, the decision was taken that the coach body rebuild should wait until the power bogie was well advanced. Project members did not want to rebuild the coach and then find that the power bogie and the boiler would not fit into the body or worse still, there was not a power bogie at all.

Experience gained elsewhere, especially with the painstaking rebuild of No. 6023 *King Edward II*, which in many ways is all but a new locomotive, showed that that while engineering drawings may be accurate, when items come to be fitted together, there can often be a discrepancy between what is on paper and what is in reality.

A member of the project team, the late Ralph Tutton, had located and catalogued a sizeable number of original drawings and documents relating to the GWR railmotors, thereby providing a base on which the project could build.

Yet there were inevitably still going to be sceptics who would maintain it couldn't be done. To cover every base, the project team spent nearly five years carrying out an enormous amount

Auto-trailer No. 212 on display at Didcot for the launch of the steam railmotor project in April 1998.
ADRIAN KNOWLES

of work behind the scenes to ensure it was viable before launching the scheme in public so serious fundraising could begin.

Despite the vast amount of material amassed by Ralph Tutton, there were still gaps in the necessary knowledge for building the new steam bogie. Most significantly, there were no surviving drawings of the motion to be found. Draughtsmen Mike Rudge and Sam Espley set to work recalculating everything from known dimensions.

By early 1997, a blueprint for restoration had been drawn up. It was estimated that the railmotor could be rebuilt for £440,000, and the society decided to apply to the Heritage Lottery Fund. However, the HLF has a demarcation line in that its aim is to save existing artefacts, not build replicas. So while the coach body would qualify at a later date, the new steam bogie would not.

Undeterred, the society decided to focus its efforts of building what had already been recognised as the single most important item – the steam bogie – while looking at exploring different avenues for fundraising.

The project was publicly launched at Didcot in April 1998 and many people responded by coming forward to either offer financial help or assistance in kind.

Dennis Howells, owner of Western Region pannier tank No. 9466, was appointed project manager for the power bogie and held talks with Bob Meanley, chief engineer at Birmingham Railway Museum, which had an engineering base firmly in GWR territory at Tyseley shed, and which had played a crucial role in the early stages of the building of The A1 Steam Locomotive Trust's £3-million Peppercorn A1 Pacific No. 60163 *Tornado*. It was agreed that the main frame of the steam bogie would be erected at Tyseley Locomotive Works.

RESTORATION BEGINS

Meanwhile, initial work on the coach body began one weekend in 1999. Volunteers at Didcot removed the external steel panelling that had been fitted when the coach was converted to an auto-trailer.

Digging out the puttied screw heads and easing the rusted threads, the team removed the metal panels one by one to reveal the original 1908 hardwood frame, and it was found to the delight of all that that apart from some rot in the solebars and areas where the roof had been leaking, the 91-year-old frame was in excellent condition for its age.

Because the original wooden panelling had been thicker than the steel panels of the 1930s, the GWR had fitted spacer pieces to make up the difference. These kept the steel panels away from the frame and away from moisture and condensation that had run down inside the void over the decades.

Graham Drew, who had been appointed project manager for the vehicle body, found himself also facing a lack of historical information. Very few detailed drawings relating to the myriad

Stripping the panels of the coach body in 1999. ADRIAN KNOWLES

of smaller parts required existed, so he had to produce new manufacturing specifications for almost everything, working from photographic evidence and cross referencing to drawings of other vehicles. There were no detailed drawings of the boiler compartment, for example.

The interior construction of the compartment was therefore redesigned by reference to GWR custom and practice in coach and wagon construction, and relying to some extent on using photographs from the exterior. In so many ways, the railmotor was being designed and re-engineered by the society from informed scratch.

THE NEW STEAM BOGIE ON WHEELS

The building of the power bogie received an early boost when a society member sponsored the manufacture of the frames. A total of 700 holes needed to be drilled in the steelwork and these were riveted up and fitted together for completion in 2000.

At the same time, Ken Gibbs, who had for many years made patterns for the broad gauge

Fire Fly replica, switched to producing patterns for the new bogie to what in his British Railways days had been his old office!

An early pattern produced by Ken was for the driving wheels. The GWR railmotor bogies had at various times run with wheelsets of three different diameters – 3ft 6in, 3ft 8in and 4ft.

The society decided that No. 93's new bogie would have 4ft diameter wheelsets, but much care had to be taken with cross checking against other dimensions on the drawings to ensure that everything else fitted accordingly.

Responsibility for overseeing the manufacture of the new wheelsets was undertaken by Dennis Howells and Mike Rudge, who had undertaken the production of the first new standard gauge wheelset in preservation with *King Edward II's* new trailing driving wheels and were heavily involved at the time with the five new wheelsets for the new Saint project.

Tackling these jobs back-to-back, the society arranged for the manufacture of the railmotor's new wheelsets to coincide with those for the Saint, giving the project a huge uplift in the credibility stakes.

The wheels were, like those for the Saint, cast at William Cook Ltd of Burton-on-Trent and sent to Bootham Engineering of Weedon, Northamptonshire, for machining.

In February 2003 the wheelsets, including the return crank assemblies, were completed at Weedon and delivered to Tyseley, where, in November 2000, the bogie mainframe had been erected, with other key components, including the motion brackets, underkeeps, horn guides and guard irons, machined and fitted to the frames shortly afterwards.

The project team had seized on a highly-competitive foundry quote, and both cylinder blocks for the railmotor were cast in the first half of 2001, together with the steam chest and front and back cylinder covers.

The right-hand cylinder assembly was fully machined and fitted to the chassis first to enable measurements to be taken in connection with the design of the motion. In addition the motion brackets were fitted on both sides. Once everything had been proved, the second cylinder was machined.

The axleboxes were cast in 2002 and machined to fit the new wheelsets before being fitted into the new hornguides which had been attached to the bogie.

The four main springs were manufactured by a Sheffield firm and the remaining spring gear arrived by air freight from Australia at Christmas 2003 having been made by Lovells Springs of Paramatta, Sydney.

These joined the power bogie frame and the four axleboxes and permitted the assembly of a rolling chassis for the first time during summer 2003. Everyone could now see that the project was taking shape big time, and that it really was possible to recreate a steam railmotor, the forgotten vehicle of the steam age.

The driving end of the coach body in September 2004. ADRIAN KNOWLES

The frame for the new steam bogie. ADRIAN KNOWLES

Project leader Dennis Howells with the smokebox in April 2004. ADRIAN KNOWLES

The new vertical boiler at Israel Newton & Sons in April 2004. ADRIAN KNOWLES

BUILDING THE BOILER

With the chassis at an advanced stage, attention turned to the biggest job of all on any new-build project – the boiler.

It appears that the GWR sold railmotor boilers out of traffic for industrial or private use and several people contacted the society with suggestions of where one might still exist. These ranged from a school in Southampton and premises in Chester, but they turned out to be false trails.

Even if a railmotor boiler had survived, it must be doubtful whether it would have been capable of being restored.

Some members suggested adapting an existing vertical boiler, maybe one from a crane.

However, it was soon decided that a new boiler would have to be built to the correct original specification, even if it would cost £90,000 as some members feared.

The society was fortunate in having a set of original 1904 drawings for the boiler and Gordon Newton, sixth-generation proprietor of boilermakers Israel Newton & Sons of Bradford which had made the boiler for *Fire Fly*, was therefore a first choice for the society.

A decision was taken at the outset that despite the extra cost, the firebox should be copper

Far left: *The boiler and smokebox in September 2007.* ADRIAN KNOWLES

Left: *The new water tank for the railmotor.* ADRIAN KNOWLES

since this would last longer than a steel firebox and be more likely to be able to cope with corrosion which might arise from the less frequent use.

Gordon quoted just £57,000 to build a traditional riveted boiler with a copper firebox.

Thanks to a sizeable financial input from the Esmée Fairbairn Foundation, which provided around 25 per cent of the total cost of the boiler and its peripherals, the society was able to go ahead.

Manufacture began in 2003 and the boiler shell and all the fittings were completed at the end of 2005. Simultaneously with the construction of the boiler, work was also progressing on the manufacture of a complete set of boiler fittings again to the early twentieth-century design. This was also a lengthy business since patterns did not exist for many of the fittings and had to be made before they could be cast and machined. The new fittings were gradually gathered together and delivered to Bradford to be fitted to the boiler.

With the new ashpan, grate, chimney and smokebox manufactured, the boiler underwent a successful hydraulic test in May 2006. The total cost of the boiler and all of its fittings was estimated at around £100,000.

TACKLING THE COACH BODY

With the completion of the steam bogie well on track, thoughts switched to the coach body. Because the Didcot workshops were full to capacity with other carriage restoration projects, 15 outside contractors were invited to tender for the project.

Graham Drew, a marine engineer with the Ministry of Defence, saw that many of the skills called for in restoring the railmotor body were available in shipyards. Among the organisations invited to tender were the Royal Naval Dockyard, Devonport, and Fleet Support Limited, Portsmouth as well as traditional railway contractors. A highly-detailed specification

Restoring the railmotor's droplight windows in September 2010. GRAHAM DREW

was dawn up and personnel from the tendering contractors visited Didcot to carry out intensive surveys of the railmotor, a task made easier by the removal of the 1930s panels.

Together with the specifications and submissions for educational and interpretation facilities, the quotations obtained enabled an entirely new application to the Heritage Lottery Fund , for the restoration of the vehicle body and underframe, which were classed as surviving artefacts and not new build. The steam bogie would be excluded from the application, but brought into the Lottery bid was Didcot's 1912-built auto-trailer No. 92. Another great survivor, this unusual 70ft panelled vehicle, which had been built with a corridor connection at the luggage end, had been designed to work with the steam railmotors as one of the earliest forms of multiple unit train. At an early stage of the project it was considered that the trailer should also be restored, to run as a pair with the railmotor in the twenty-first century.

No. 92 was built at Swindon in 1912 to Diagram U, Lot 1198, and is similar in appearance and construction to No. 93, although varying considerably in detail.

The trailer was withdrawn in January 1957 and used initially as a mess room by GKN workmen in Cardiff Docks. It was acquired by the society in 1969 and was originally stored at Swindon, moving to the society's Taunton depot in 1972, and finally to Didcot in 1977. There, it was used for several years as staff accommodation at Didcot and without the railmotor project, may have waited decades for restoration in its own right, if ever.

The new Lottery bid which took Graham 18 months to prepare stressed the huge educational aspect of recreating a forerunner of today's modern trains. Running to more than 150 pages, it was submitted on Friday 13 October 2006.

SITTING DOWN DOWN UNDER

Another problem facing both Nos. 92 and 93 was the lack of authentic seats, both having lost their originals long ago. Like the railmotor, the trailer had also been converted for Departmental use, all interior fittings and fixtures being removed to provide open plan accommodation.

When faced with a similar problem in the case of GWR auto-trailer No. 190, new seats were fabricated from aged oak obtained from old church pews. However, many of the seats in the railmotor and its trailer were the steel-framed 'walkover' type, popular in tramcars in which the back could be flipped so that passengers could choose to face either direction.

The style of seat fitted by the GWR was patented by Henry Hale of Philadelphia, USA, and manufactured by Hale & Kilburn in Chicago, New York and Philadelphia, as well as under licence in the UK by G. D. Peters & Co whose works stood alongside the GWR main line at Slough. The firm's site was rail connected, and delivery of seats to Swindon would have been easy.

Early on in the project, society members ran the rule over surplus tram seats from Blackpool

The specially-woven fabric for the window blinds. ROBIN JONES

Above left: *The Glenelg tram in Australia which provided the correct seats for the railmotor, with Mario Mencigar, the scrap dealer who sold the redundant seats to the GWS, and GWS members Reg Watters (centre) and John Moore (right).* GWS Above right: *A Glenelg tram in service, Adelaide, November 2001.* ALDO DELICATA

Tramway vehicles but they were found not only to be in very poor condition but in need to extensive adaptation to bring them anywhere near the railmotor type.

Research showed that the required type of seats had been used by the Swansea & Mumbles Railway in its tramcars.

The only item surviving from any of those vehicles was one seat currently on display in The Tramshed, part of Swansea Museum.

Arrangements were made to borrow this seat so that a new set of drawings could be made and a fresh batch of the seats ordered.

A report of this 'find' published in the society's newsletter, and in what was viewed as a preservation miracle, society members John Moore and Reg Watters who were living in Australia quickly identified a source of genuine G.D. Peters walkover seats on some 1929-built tramcars that were being withdrawn from the Glenelg Tramway in Adelaide. It was found that the seats were exactly the type required, and John and Reg bargained hard to obtain 40 of them – enough for both Nos. 92 and 93.

The seats were reimported to England and retired London banker Alan Moore, a major financial benefactor to the heritage railway sector, helped out by funding the transport cost. The seats were subsequently repainted, modified to remove a handle in the walkover back which the GW seats did not have, and reupholstered in the correct brown and white moquette which was specially woven for the project.

One of the refurbished seats. GRAHAM DREW

THE FIRST STEAMINGS

Meanwhile, Dennis Howells was honing the steam bogie to perfection. Many new fittings had been made, including the brake valve, regulator, and gauge glass assembly.

By January 2007, these were bolted to the boiler which was steam tested for the first time, at Israel Newton's works in All Alone Road on the outskirts of Bradford.

Smoke belched from the roof of the works, while inside, smoke and steam filled the air and the roar from the safety valves was deafening.

As the pressure rose, Gordon Newton adjusted the safety valves until they were just 'feathering' at the working pressure of 160psi. The first heritage era British-built boiler for a new standard gauge engine had well and truly arrived.

After the successful steam test, the boiler was drained and dried out so that its ten-year ticket would not start: that would wait until it would be attached to the steam bogie for running-in trials.

WINNING THE LOTTERY!

Another major victory came in July 2007 when the Heritage Lottery Fund announced £768,500 was awarded for the restoration of the original timber bodies and steel underframes of both the railmotor and trailer No 92.

The successful tender was submitted by the award-winning carriage workshops of the Llangollen Railway.

However, first of all, the railmotor and its trailer had to return to the main line!

Because there is no road access to Didcot Railway Centre, there is only one way to move the society's rolling stock in and out, and that is by rail from nearby Milton sidings. However, vehicles moved over the national rail network first have to be certified that they are capable of such movements.

Right: *Cladding the railmotor body.*
ADRIAN KNOWLES

Far right: *The railmotor body arrives by low loader in September 2007.*
GRAHAM DREW

A series of inspections and more than five miles of trial running on Didcot's demonstration line were held in order to prove that the railmotor and trailer could be moved without falling apart on the way. The railmotor was duly registered as No. 99093 and the trailer as No. 99092 in the Network Rail stock register.

The pair were finally moved to Milton on 4 September 2007. From there, both vehicles were taken by road on low-loaders and arrived at Llangollen three days later.

Dave Owen, Llangollen's engineering manager, and his team of fitters and apprentices quickly got to grips with the project and within weeks the body of No. 93 had been lifted on jacks and cross beams from the underframe and work started on restoration, together with the mechanical modifications required to convert the underframes back to a railmotor configuration. A new water tank and a complete set of brake gear were manufactured to replace missing items. The main structural steelwork on the underframe was replaced where corrosion was found, and the coach bogie was fully overhauled.

Despite their very worn condition, the body of steam railmotor No. 93 and its trailer, No. 92, had to be main line certified to be taken out of Didcot Railway Centre, for the only access for vehicles is by rail. With the giant cooling towers of Didcot power station in the distance, they are moved out behind a Class 66 on 4 September 2007 for the short trip to Milton sidings before being transferred to a low loader for onward shipment to Llangollen. ADRIAN KNOWLES

The assembled power bogie at Tyseley in November 2007. ADRIAN KNOWLES

A WORLD IN MOTION

Meanwhile, at Tyseley, Bob Meanley's men were also busy. The boiler had been delivered from Israel Newton and was united with the bogie chassis for the first time on 27 November 2007.

In March 2008, the steam bogie and boiler were moved to Didcot where they were displayed for the rest of the year to boost project awareness.

Still there was much research that needed to be done before anything could move.

With regard to the thorny problem of the motion, Mike Rudge had been struggling with some of the finer dimensions of the valve gear, due to the above-mentioned absence of original drawings.

A stoke of luck came with the realisation that the three Vale of Rheidol 2-6-2 tank engines, which has been built at Swindon during 1923/4 after the GWR had inherited the Aberystwyth to Devil's Bridge line, were found to have very similar motion, and thereby provided Mike with a solution.

He was able to produce a new set of drawings, but just to make sure that he was on the right track before the final motion parts were manufactured, some dummy parts were made in timber by Roger Paddison.

Then, to the amazement of all, at the eleventh hour, a set of original motion drawings were found at the National Railway Museum by society members looking for drawings for the County Project. They confirmed that Mike's calculations were less than a hair's breadth away from being spot on, and so the go ahead was given for the last motion parts to be forged.

Right: *The mocked-up wooden motion parts.* ADRIAN KNOWLES

Far right: *The underframe being shotblasted.* GRAHAM DREW

In early 2009, the power bogie assembly arrived at Llangollen, where Dave Owen's team completed the machining of the motion and fittings, manufactured the boiler pipework and controls before the completed assembly was united with the restored underframe for the first time. This assembly underwent test running before the underframe went back beneath the railmotor body in the carriage workshops where the connecting pipework and vehicle controls were manufactured and fitted.

TRIAL RUNS AT LLANGOLLEN

With valve setting on the power bogie complete by autumn 2010, the whole power bogie unit was finally assembled and fitted with temporary platforms fore and aft to facilitate steam test running.

A visually very unusual set of test runs took place at Llangollen on 17 November. The power bogie, looking every bit like a pioneer locomotive from the very early days of steam railways, ran on its own up and down the line to Pentrefelin. It worked perfectly, and emitted a crisp, mellow exhaust beat.

One of the strangest steam locomotive movements ever seen on a British railway: the steam power bogie being taken for test runs on the Llangollen Railway minus the railmotor body!
ADRIAN KNOWLES

The boiler being lifted into the body of No. 93. ADRIAN KNOWLES

On 23 November, the steam bogie was finally rolled beneath the body of No. 93.
The boiler was craned in through the engine compartment roof, and the net result – a complete steam railmotor!

THE FINEST DETAILS RESTORED

While the mechanical restoration was progressing over a two year period, Dave's team of coach builders worked at repanelling No. 93's body inside and out, completing the floors and roof, together with the enormous task of making and fitting all the exterior and interior mouldings.

The complete boiler end of the body was rebuilt from scratch to replace the end modified on conversion to a trailer in 1936, and new exterior doors were manufactured and fitted together with installation of the famous Australian seats.

As well as overseeing the restoration of the coach body, Graham Drew also had responsibility for sourcing or producing the thousands of parts and fittings, from the 450-gallon water tank down to the pull to open signs on each of the window ventilators.

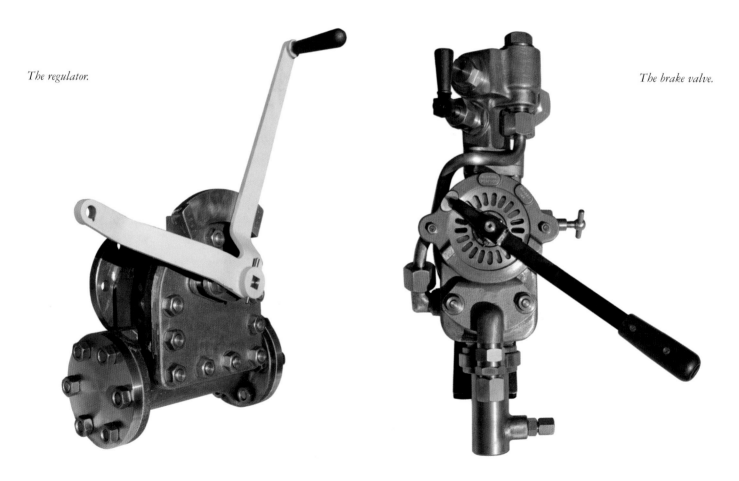

The regulator.

The brake valve.

The communications bell.

Ventilator tag.

Caution notice.

Letter rack.

Ticket box.

Suggs gas lamp.

Period light.

Vacuum gauge.

Pressure gauge.

Roof ventilator

Door handles.

It was decided from the outset that no corners would be cut, and everything would be recreated to the finest detail. Working gas lamps were a non-starter due to health and safety considerations, but Sugg Lighting Ltd produced a series of electrically-powered replicas. Graham himself co-ordinated the input from over a hundred different contractors as well as manufacturing some components in his own workshop.

An example of how far the society was prepared to go in recreating the original as far as possible is evident in the fabric for the window blinds, a complex design featuring a GWR monogram which was produced by the Nederlands Textielmuseum in Holland, one of the few places that can still undertake this specialised weaving.

FINAL ASSEMBLY COMPLETED

Over the winter of 2010/11, pipework, mechanical linkages, fitting out and painting were undertaken, with the epic first movement of the completed vehicle being undertaken during the evening of Sunday 27 February – the first time it had moved under its own power since November 1934. The following day a successful full trial run was undertaken before No. 93 was returned to works for final painting and lining out.

It was decided not, in the first instance, to paint the railmotor in the familiar and much-loved GWR livery of chocolate and cream which they carried in later years. Instead, a brave but hugely-commendable decision was made to go for the largely-forgotten previous GWR livery of 1912-22, crimson lake lined in gold with a white roof. Inside, the saloons are a mix of scumbled panels and varnished trim with ridged hardwood flooring and brass fittings.

Lining out, painting the crests and lettering, together with the interior scumbling, was undertaken by local craftsman David Kynaston who normally paints canal boats.

One of the first trial runs at Llangollen in late February 2011.
ADRIAN KNOWLES

CHAPTER SEVEN

BACK IN SERVICE

ON COMPLETION OF painting, No. 93 finally entered traffic on Monday 21 March, carrying a party of project supporters from Llangollen to Carrog and back. At Carrog, GWS chairman Richard Croucher gave a speech thanking everyone who had been involved in the restoration project.

No. 93 then took part in a series of fundraising photo charters over the Llangollen Railway for three days. Participants were blessed with glorious spring sunshine as the railmotor,

No.93 passes the farmstead of Garth-y-Dwr with spring in full bloom on 22 March 2011. ROBIN JONES

Resplendent in its original livery of GWR crimson lake, reborn steam railmotor No. 93 takes the Llangollen Railway by storm on 22 March 2011. ROBIN JONES

No. 93 meets the Llangollen Railway's award-winning restored 1958-built Wickham two-car DMU No.56171, one of the first generation DMU types produced by private companies and a direct descendant. ROBIN JONES

Replenishing the firebox in a slightly more cramped space than on the usual tank engine! ROBIN JONES

No. 93 rests at Carrog. It is believed that it may have run on the Ruabon-Barmouth route, part of which is now the Llangollen Railway, in GWR days. ROBIN JONES

believed to have run on the Ruabon-Barmouth route in GWR days, posed for pictures at a series of classic locations.

Nobody who saw or travelled on No. 93 could have anything but praise. There had been some scepticism as to whether the railmotor would fall between two stools – too diesel-like for steam fans and too antiquated for modern traction enthusiasts, while being a non-starter for the general public whose grandparents may not have been born when the last GWR example was in service. As the completed project was showered with accolades about the fine detail of its finish, the authentic recreation of fittings and features both inside and out, its superb ride and unique charisma, all three assumptions were proved wrong.

The railmotor returned to its home depot at Didcot on 4 April 2011. The free space in the carriage and wagon workshop at Llangollen was then occupied by trailer No. 92 and work commenced on restoring that vehicle to the same high standard.

On Friday 29 April, No. 93 ran for the first time at Didcot to check clearances with

Opposite: Picking up a head of steam in the Dee Valley. ROBIN JONES

The replication of the original crest is a work of art. ROBIN JONES

Above: *Few design concessions to modern safety standards include the use of electric lighting instead of the original gas lamps.* ROBIN JONES

Above left: *Loading the luggage as would have been done in the early twentieth century.* ADRIAN KNOWLES

Left: *The brand new vertical boiler – the beating heart.* ROBIN JONES

Below: *Clear road ahead: a driver's view from the cab of No. 93.* ROBIN JONES

Heading westwards to Glyndyfrdwy.
ROBIN JONES

The hills are alive…with the sound of a railmotor! ROBIN JONES

platforms and other structures on the site, in preparation for its public launch on Saturday 28 May, when it offered rides to the general public for the first time.

It was officially launched into traffic on the centre turntable by Adrian Shooter, chairman of main line operator Chiltern Railways, and who has his own 2ft gauge Beeches Light Railway at his home in Oxfordshire.

Afterwards, visitors were able to photograph a unique line-up in front of the running shed which marked the evolution of the self-contained self-propelled train over more than a century: the essence of this book.

On the far left stood GWR steam railmotor No. 93, while on the far right saw the 2011 'equivalent' – an 'out of the box' gleaming white new Chiltern Railways Class 172 Turbostar, delivered to the company just two days before and never used by passengers. In between, in chronological order stood four vehicles which completed a unique evolutionary chain between the pair.

Next to the railmotor stood Collett auto-tank No. 4866 with a carmine-and-cream auto-trailer. To its right was GWR diesel railcar No. 22, and next to that was a Class 122 'bubblecar', No. 121034, which, after three years out of service, was repainted in BR green livery, and which earlier had offered short passenger rides. Next was First Great Western Class 166 Turbo train No. 166215.

The same day, Joyce Hancock, aunt of the late Great Western Society expert Charles Whetmath, cut the ribbon to open the centre's new railmotor shed.

Charles died three years previously and left a legacy to the GWS, which was used to build the replica of the corrugated-iron railmotor shed that stood at Southall in GWR days. It has been named the Charles Whetmath Building in his honour.

On Saturday 11 June, the railmotor lined up at Didcot alongside the most famous new build locomotive of them all to date – the visiting A1 Peppercorn Pacific No. 60163 *Tornado*, which took The A1 Steam Locomotive Trust 18 years to build at Tyseley and Darlington, at

Would we dare have plush moquette like this on seats in a suburban train of the twenty-first century? ROBIN JONES

The interior of long-scrapped sister railmotor No. 87, highlighting the amazing replication job done on No. 93 internally as well as on the outside. GWS

The launch party at Didcot on 28 May 2011: left to right: Dennis Howells (project engineer, power bogie); Graham Drew (project engineer, vehicle body and underframe); Adrian Shooter CBE (chairman, Chiltern Railways); Richard Croucher (chairman Great Western Society); Mike Rudge (design engineer and draughtsman); Sam Espley (draughtsman).

Watched by GWS chairman Richard Croucher, Adrian Shooter officially launches steam railmotor No. 93. ROBIN JONES

Steam railmotor No. 93 breaks the ribbon following its official launch by Chiltern Railways chairman Adrian Shooter. ROBIN JONES

The replica of Southall's original steam railmotor shed at Didcot: No. 93 is not only restored but has a home of its own! FRANK DUMBLETON

a cost of £3-million and which was launched on to the main line in late January 2009. Having had the honour of hauling the Royal Train that spring after being officially launched into traffic by Prince Charles, and been given a starring role in BBC2's *Top Gear* programme when it raced a vintage car and motorbike from London to Edinburgh, *Tornado* continues to generate headlines and draw crowds wherever it goes.

Once trailer No. 92 is ready, both it and No. 93 are likely to be painted in the GWR's later railmotor livery of the more familiar chocolate and cream. The pair will then tour many of Britain's heritage lines, several of which once had railmotor services in Edwardian times. The South Devon, Gloucestershire Warwickshire and Bodmin & Wenford railways will no doubt be paid a visit, and an exhaustive set of 'authentic' destination boards has been made.

It no doubt will be a star turn at gala events, a curiosity in itself. However, its greatest value lies in the field of education, for at last we have the missing bridge which truly links the trains we regularly use today with the fabulous period of technological innovation that was the steam age.

And as a trip back in time, to appreciate the exquisite elegance of Edwardian railways, No. 93 can be bettered only by a Tardis.

Joyce Hancock, aunt of the late Great Western Society expert Charles Whetmath, cuts the ribbon to open the centre's new railmotor shed. Charles died three years before and left a legacy to the GWS, which has been used to build the replica of the railmotor shed that once stood at Southall. It has been named the Charles Whetmath Building. FRANK DUMBLETON

CHAPTER EIGHT
THE MIDDLETON MILESTONE

BASED IN HARROGATE, coach restorer Stephen Middleton had built up a reputation for restoring vintage vehicles which other groups shied away from as too difficult. In one instance, he even sold a prize collection of Hornby Dublo trains and horse dung to pay for carriage restoration. On the Embsay & Bolton Abbey Steam Railway in Yorkshire, his Victorian wooden-bodied saloons run under the banner of Stately Trains.

However, while the Great Western Society was making tangible steps with steam railmotor No. 93, Stephen had his eye on the 'other' missing link – North Eastern railway petrol-electric autocar No. 3170.

As stated earlier, its body had been pensioned off as a holiday bungalow, which by the twenty-first century was in a state of disrepair, although a tin roof had shielded it from the elements. In September 2003, Stephen bought it from the landowner, and moved it to join his other vehicles at Embsay.

The following year, he drew together six experts from other heritage lines who shared his vision – another 'project impossible just like No. 93 – of restoring the autocar as near as possible to its rebuilt 1923 condition, and operational too.

They formed the North Eastern Railway 1903 Electric Autocar Trust and set about sourcing suitable components for the project, designing its rebuild and most importantly, fundraising to make it happen.

Firstly, the body needed serious attention. When sold off by the LNER, it had been cut in two halves to facilitate its journey by road. Window pillars needed to be repaired and the body structure completely overhauled.

Early on, a suitable underframe was secured from the LNER Coach Association. Plans were drawn up to have them re-engineered to take the new engine, generator, traction motors and control equipment.

However, as with the GWR steam railmotor project, obviously the most important component if it was to be anything other than a static museum piece was to be a new

Autocar No. 3170 at Embsay today, carrying NER livery and undergoing restoration to full working order. AUTOCAR TRUST

Robin Taylor's O gauge model of how the restored NER autocar and its trailer will look. KEIGHLEY MODEL RAILWAY CLUB

motor bogie.

Despite the vehicle's paramount importance to world transport history, modern regulations would not allow the use of an old petrol engine, so a diesel alternative, while not authentic, was sourced as a second-best option.

A suitable motor bogie was identified, from a Southern Region Class 416 (2EPB) EMU, and brought to Embsay. As built, No. 3170, had been fitted with a Fox power bogie, but none of these have survived.

The big advantage of using the Class 416 bogie is that both it and its motors are compatible with modern diesel generators and control equipment.

How the railcar looked after its retrieval from a site where it had been used as a bungalow for 70 years. AUTOCAR TRUST

The renovation of the interior of the autocar well underway. AUTOCAR TRUST

The bogie received a major overhaul in 2003 and has seen little use since.

Similar EE507 traction motors are still in service, so spares would be obtainable should they be needed.

The other bogie for the autocar will be an authentic Fox lightweight version. Enough of these survived for the trust to secure some for the restoration.

While, as with the GWR railmotor, the interior will be restored to its original specification, with upholstered reversible seats and guard's compartment/vestibule, in the case of No. 3170, both driving positions will be replaced with modern control equipment in old tram-style control columns.

Just as the GWR project had a suitable trailer for its railmotor, so the petrol autocar restoration scheme has obtained a matching autocoach.

No. 3453, a clerestory coach which was built by the North Eastern Railway in 1904, was converted to a driving trailer in 1906. The control equipment was removed in 1921 and in 1952 it became a mobile office. It was bought for preservation in 1971 and stored for many

Preparatory work on the replacement motor bogie. AUTOCAR TRUST

years at Levisham on the North Yorkshire Moors Railway. In 2006, the North Eastern Railway Carriage Association decided to donate it to the autocar project. It too will be fitted with Fox lightweight bogies, as sufficient examples of them have survived.

As with No. 3170, the body will be thoroughly restored to original NER condition with a driving compartment at one end, this will be fitted with through control so that the autocar and autocoach can be coupled together to form an Edwardian multiple unit which can be driven from either end, so no "running round" will be needed when the train changes direction.

Although the autocar and autocoach were unlikely to have ever run together, photographs show No 3170 in 1923 pulling a similar coach.

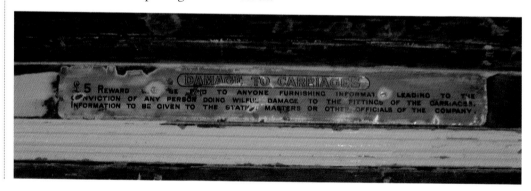

A new cab front for the petrol-electric autocar was installed on 5 July 2011. SIMON GOTT

The addition of the 58-seater vehicle will give the pair a combined capacity of 106 seats. The two vehicles will also allow passengers to appreciate the difference between the "old" type of steam era carriage with compartments and the "new" open saloon accommodation of the autocar and modern trains.

As the GWR steam railmotor team and indeed that of any new-build locomotive scheme will vouch, the key to the success of any hugely-ambitious project like this is money.

Ironically, on the same day that the completed No. 93 was unveiled to supporters at Llangollen, the Heritage Lottery Fund awarded £465,800 to the NER autocar project.

The money will be used to fit a new engine, generator, controls and brakes to the railcar, so it can enter service within a year or two.

The award covered the completion of the refurbishment of the bodywork of both No 3170 and its trailer.

Other grant aid came from the Ken Hoole Trust and PRISM (The Fund for the Preservation of Industrial and Scientific Material).

Stephen said: "The train, when finished, will be fully accessible to all, and equipped with the latest audio visual techniques will act as a 'mobile classroom' for schools and community groups so they can learn all about the development of rail transport from steam travel, to the present day."

The NER autocar set will be a perfect northern counterpoint to the GWR steam railmotor in the south. When completed, it will not only run on its 'home' line at Embsay but will also tour other heritage railways, like the North Yorkshire Moors Railway.

There is also an excellent chance that it will meet up with the steam railmotor, maybe at a special gala event. There will always be the friendly rivalry for bragging rights: the steam railmotor concept came first, but the autocar was built five years before No. 93, so which has the greater importance in the grand scheme of railway history?

Together the pair will illustrate the fact that while the development of the steam locomotive had yet to reach anything like its peak when they were designed, they were sowing the seeds that grew into the modern multiple-unit-dominated railway network of today, and indeed, that modern trains were running more than a century ago.

Not only has the 'rediscovery' of both railcars restored an important new dimension to popular railway history, but has also rewritten it. Each now unique, their heritage and educational value is priceless beyond compare.

CHAPTER NINE
OTHER RAILMOTORS STILL WITH US

THANKS TO THE STERLING efforts of the Great Western Society and Stephen Middleton, we now not only have an Edwardian steam railmotor and petrol-electric autocar, but when their trailers are completed, we will have a British Steam Multiple Unit and the world's first 'DMU', even if it was originally fuelled by petrol.

It is hard to imagine any other group taking on further similar projects of seemingly-impossible proportions, but many miracles have been worked in railway preservation since volunteers took over the Talyllyn Railway in 1951, and nothing can be ruled out.

It would certainly be possible to follow the example of No. 93 and recreate another railmotor using an authentic body. Locomotion: the National Railway Museum at Shildon has amongst its stored collection the body of a Midland Railway steam railmotor, No. 2234.

Built at Derby to Diagram 479, lot No. 578 in 1904, it was converted into an officers' saloon in 1907, but retained its engine until 1917. The four-wheeler was subsequently converted to an ordinary coach and later used in Departmental service.

It was bought for preservation in 1968 by railway historian George Dow and moved to a siding at Machynlleth where it was used as a holiday home, but was vandalised while on the site. It was sold to the National Railway Museum in 1977.

Although the structural condition is said to be poor, it still has its original bogies, underframe and running gear, while externally it is very much as built. It too is considered to be of exceptional historical importance – and there are already those who would like to see it follow in the footsteps of No. 93.

In 2001, readers of *Heritage Railway* magazine contributed towards the securing of the wooden body of the coach section of one of the two 1905-built steam railmotors built for the Great North of Scotland Railway, which was rediscovered in use as a store on a farm near Aberdeen. When redundant coaches were withdrawn at Inverurie Works, they were sold off to local farmers for use as stores, outbuildings or chicken coops.

The find was viewed as particularly significant for Scottish railway heritage as the country

Great Southern & Western Railway 0-6-0T No. 90 was part of a 'carriage engine' until 1915. ROBERT GARDINER/DCDR

The Didcot team that undertook driver training in Swiss railcar CZm 1/2 31: left to right, John Minchin, Graham Drew, Peter Jennings and Mark Baldry. GWS

135

fared comparatively badly with other areas of the UK mainland in terms of steam locomotive preservation, as the country never had the benefit of a benevolent scrapman like Dai Woodham of Barry who famously gave redundant steam locomotives a breathing space of many years until they could be bought for preservation.

The body of the railmotor was moved by Royal Deeside Railway Preservation Society volunteers and is now in safe storage under sheeting at their depot in Aberdeen waiting for the day that it may be restored in one form or another.

The GNoSR railmotors were numbered 29 and 31, but it remains unclear as to which one is the survivor.

The surviving but dilapidated trailer of one of the three Jersey Railway Sentinel steam railmotors which ran until the 1930s has in recent times been moved from the island's Pallot Steam Museum to Belgium to be rebuilt.

As we saw in Chapter One, No. 90, a 'carriage engine' from Ireland's Great Southern & Western Railway converted to a regular 0-6-0T in 1915 survives at the Downpatrick & County Down Railway. The venue also has the 50ft body of 1905-built Belfast & County

Operational Swiss steam railcar CZm 1/2 31 crosses a public road tram style. GWS

Down Railway steam railmotor No. 2 which lost its Kitson locomotive section in 1918/19 and which is now being restored to its latter-day incarnation as auto-coach No. 72.

The carriage was discovered in a field in Gilford in County Armagh in the late 1980s, being used as a house. When the owner passed away, his family donated the carriage body to the DCDR. Work began on the restoration project in 2007, with the vehicle fitted on to a former Great Southern & Western Railway underframe, and structural

The repatriated Egyptian State Railways Sentinel Steam Multiple Unit at Quainton Road. ROBIN JONES

137

work to unify the body which had been cut in half for transport when the carriage was sold in the 1950s.

Despite the withdrawal of its steam railcars from the British main line, Sentinel still had a ready market overseas. It supplied around 80 narrow gauge versions to different parts of the world, including Australia and Tasmania, India, Newfoundland and South America. It also supplied the only RM class Sentinel-Cammell steam railcar run by the New Zealand Railways Department.

In 1951, Sentinel built ten steam railcars for the Egyptian National Railways. One of them, a Steam Multiple Unit, has been repatriated and is now stored in non-serviceable condition at

The operation Sentinel steam railcar at Sri Lanka's National Railway Museum. RER JAYASRI RUWANPURA

The remains of the coach body of one of the two Great North of Scotland Railway steam railmotors protected by sheeting. ROYAL DEESIDE RAILWAY

the Buckinghamshire Railway Centre at Quainton Road. It is an articulated unit with three carriage bodies sharing four bogies, rather than the six in a traditional three-car multiple unit.

Three out of six 2ft 6in gauge Sentinel steam railmotors supplied to Sir Lanka in 1927/28 survive at the country's National Railway Museum in Olcott Mawatha, Colombo. One of them, No. 331, is in full working order and is paraded as the world's sole surviving narrow gauge steam railmotor. If the museum never intends to use the other two, what a wonderful repatriation project a surplus one would make!

When the Great Western Society steam railmotor crew began learning how to drive such a vehicle, before it was completed, they flew to Switzerland to take the controls of surviving steam railcar CZm 1/2 31. Built by Maschinenfabrik Esslinge in 1902 for SBB (Swiss Federal Railways) and sold five years later to the Uerikon-Bauma-Bahn, it is now part of the SBB Historic museum and operated by Dampfgruppe Zürich (steam group Zürich), and runs regular enthusiast trips over the main line.

Opposite: *The Midland Railway railmotor in Shildon's Locomotion museum: could it one day follow No. 93 in being restored?* ANTHONY COULLS

The Sentinel railcar on the Tacna to Arica Railway in South America. JAN PESULA

In 1999, the Czech Railways Museum, housed in a former engine shed of the Bušthrad Railway in Lužná u Rakovníka took over the maintenance and operation of historical rail vehicles from volunteers who had established a base there two years earlier. Its oldest operational steam exhibit is a railcar, M124.001.

The first historic vehicles were exhibited here in 1997, initially thanks to volunteer work by members of several associations concerned with railway history. In 1999 the exhibition was taken over by Czech Railways, which has been operating it as part of the Depot of Historic Vehicles up to the present day.

The coach body for the private Stortford Railway's Jersey Railway Sentinel steam railcar. PAUL BENNETT

Left: *A contemporary postcard of a Belfast & County Down Railway steam railmotor.* DCDR

Below: *The Belfast & County Down railmotor body being restored as an auto-coach.* DCDR

It was one of only two vehicles built to this design in Ringhoffer Wagon Works in Prague's Smíchov district in 1903. The boilers were supplied by Komarek Maschinenfabrik of Vienaa.

The pair were originally intended for the Czech Northern Railway to run the line Česká Lípa-Kamenický Šenov line. However, due to the steep gradients, they were purchased by then Austrian state railway kkStB and were allocated to the Nusle-Modřany, the Libochovice-Louny and the Opočno–Dobruška line, where they ran into the 1940s.

In 1949, M124.001 was given to the Technical Museum in Prague for static display, but 60 years later, was restored to running order.

The standard gauge Tacna to Arica Railway, which runs across the border from Peru to Chile has at least one Sentinel railmotor converted to diesel which was still operating in recent years. A number of Sentinel steam railcar bodies minus engines survived in Tasmania.

Finally, a steam railcar was due to return to a former part of the British national network in late 2011.

The Bishops Stortford, Dunmow & Braintree Railway, later part of the Great Eastern Railway, opened in 1864 but lost its passenger services as early as 1952, with freight lingering on ever-diminishing sections until 1972.

In the back garden of enthusiast Paul Bennett's house in Bishop's Stortford, which has been extended to include part of the old trackbed, runs the private 7¼in gauge Stortford Railway, a 120-ft-long circular line which operates battery-electric locomotives and a County Donegal Railway-style railcar, and now has no less than a miniature version of a Jersey Railway Sentinel steam railmotor being the latest addition. Occasional open days are held in aid of All Saints parish church at Hockerill.

Steam railmotors were once commonplace, but now the concept is esoteric. Thanks to those groups and individuals who have never lost sight of the importance of the original all-in-one form of traction, we are now able to tell the complete story of railways, for the first time in the preservation movement.

It is to be hoped that more projects will follow in the steps of GWR steam railmotor No. 93 and its LNER petrol-electric counterpart No. 3170 in the years to come, once they have toured the country and enlightened a public that has long since forgotten that everyday travel a century ago was in many places not all that dissimilar to today's modern trains.

*GWR steam railmotor No. 93 is one of many projects covered in *Steam's New Dawn*, also written by the author and published by Halsgrove, which covers all the new-build locomotive schemes of the UK preservation movement, big and small.